CW01652935

LNER D3 class 4–4–0 No. 2000 (ex-GNR) as running in 1948. This particular engine was normally used for railway officers' specials, and was the only member of the class restored to LNER green after 1945.
[*J. M. Jarvis*

TRAINS
'SIXTYNINE

TRAINS 'SIXTYNINE

Edited by

J. B. Snell

LONDON

IAN ALLAN

12/6

Contents

Cover Picture: A London-Glasgow Freightliner headed by Brush Type 4 No. D1866, diverted because of engineering works on the West Coast main line, leaves Blea Moor tunnel on the Settle & Carlisle line on April 29, 1967. [*Derek Cross*

© Ian Allan 1968

Published in the United Kingdom by Ian Allan Ltd, Shepperton, Surrey,
and printed by Netherwood Dalton & Co., Ltd., Huddersfield

Old Dionysius's Almanack, 1969

by "Cerberus"

Steam locomotives have struggled up the shoulder of Wild Boar Fell for a century; will the diesels of today have vanished by tomorrow? *[J. L. McIvor*

One of the difficulties of the prophet's trade these days is that such a time-lag exists between putting pen to paper and publication. These words, for instance, are being written in early March 1968 and will not see daylight until late September. Still, some of us are brave enough to run the risk of being overtaken by events, notably that splendid fellow Old Moore. He has the advantage, of course, of using the fixed and calculable motions of the stars as a guide, while I must hazard the will-o'-th'-wisps of Government and Railways Board declarations of policy; still, in making four modest gazes into the crystal ball regarding the future of the British railway system, there are some more dependable influences to rely on.

Who, incidentally, was Old Dionysius? He was Doctor Dionysius Lardner (1793-1859): an Irishman, Professor of Natural Philosophy and Astronomy at London University, F.R.S. (London and Edinburgh), author or editor of 49 publications, including "An Elementary Treatise on the Differential and Integral Calculus", several "Handbooks of Natural Philosophy", "The Cabinet Cyclopaedia" (133 volumes), etc.; who made a special study of railway policy and economics, and who published during the 1840s and 1850s details of railway costings and finance in better and more useful detail than any that have appeared since (including certain moderately notorious recent publications). A name worthy of honour.

What does 1969 hold for British Railways?

Prophecy No. 1. Traffic will go down.

The decline will be moderate in passenger traffic, which since its peak in 1959 has been declining at an average rate of 2.6% per annum; nevertheless this is a trend which nothing seems likely permanently to reverse. Time was when one could go almost anywhere by train, and more or less had to; nowadays trains no longer serve many places, and although the main-line and inter-city services are, broad and long, better than they have ever been, they cater for a smaller section of the market. Furthermore, so far as they depend on buses to feed them, they are on shaky ground. The bus has proved even less able than the stopping train to compete with the private car, and it seems likely to vanish altogether, apart from long-distance express services, in rural areas (it has already done so in the U.S.A.) while becoming, in cities, less and less dependable because of worsening economics and increasing road congestion (prophecy 1(b), by the way, is that no ameliorative measures here will have more than a slight and temporary effect). The growing number of private cars, whose operating costs are still tending to decline, and the spreading motorway network will hack away at the basic intercity business. Commuter traffic will continue to decrease in total while increasing in the peaks, as it has done for years.

But of course passenger traffic doesn't matter very much really. Railways are for carrying freight. For the last ten years B.R. freight traffic has been declining at an average rate of 3.1% per annum, measured in ton-miles, but this rate has been increasing latterly to nearer 4%. The reasons for this are multiple, and partly reflect the improvement of road freight haulage, but in part also the undependability and price of B.R. service. We all know why B.R. freight service, following the traditional pattern of operation, is expensive and unsatisfactory; a miserable compound of little unbraked wagons, cramped yards, congestion and lack of discipline. What isn't yet so obvious is that the ameliorative measures so far taken aren't working. The concentration of general freight into a few large railheads, with fleets of road vehicles doing collection and delivery over a wide area, was justified by calling in aid the general rule that large units were more efficient than small ones and that a fleet of lorries was more efficient at C & D than the equivalent number of pick-up freight trains. Both propositions are not necessarily true; it is mainly a matter of management and organization. It is, however, true as a general rule that railways, being more complicated, are more difficult to manage than (to pick an example out of the air) a factory for canning peas; and it is also true as a general rule that the calibre of their management has been one of the railway's weakest points, if only because for fifty years at least they have paid less than the market rate for brainpower and been forced as a result to promote those who knew how to operate the existing set-up because they didn't have enough people clever enough to devise a better set-up. Hence, in a nutshell, the collapse of wagonload traffic; the bread and butter of every other railway system in the world. The Liner Train has been touted as the answer to all this, basically because it is simpler and therefore easier to manage; prophecy 1(c) is that we shall continue to hear a great deal about the virtues of Liner Trains in 1969 because it will take a little longer than this for the impossibility of their living up to their billing to become sufficiently patent. They are of course an extremely good idea, but only in a small corner of the market. We may, however, start to hear a little about ordinary freight services worked with Liner Train equipment—they may even be *called* Liner Train services—and the sooner we do the better. This way traffic might start to stop declining.

Prophecy No. 2. Costs will not go down as much as revenue does.

B.R. had, in 1965-66, reached the stage where the deficit was reduced in absolute terms from one year to another in spite of a worsening ratio between expenses and receipts, simply because the undertaking had contracted faster than its operations became less profitable. Since line closures may have come to a temporary halt, more or less, there are not going to be many economies made that way for a while. I am therefore prophesying that economies will not be made in many other directions either, or not to much effect, if only because management seems to have no idea how they can be obtained.

The prosperity of Britain's railways has, till now, risen and fallen together with that of the coal industry. G.N.R. 0–8–0 No. 453 eases onto the slow road at Greenwood Box, New Barnet, with a load of house coal for London, around 1920. [*Loco. Pub. Co.*

This brash statement may surprise some. Let us therefore bow in the direction of the statistical Dionysius and give an example, not hinted at in Beeching. One Region (let it be nameless, except that since these figures refer to a London Division it is clearly not the Scottish) during autumn 1966 took the trouble to find out, by an analysis of its footplate staff's work tickets, exactly what they had been doing during a sample week. This never seems to have been done before; which, since the wage bill for enginemen on that region alone came to around £20 million per annum, may be considered surprising, but let us not chase that hare. It was discovered that, leaving firemen or second men out of the reckoning, the 300-odd drivers employed at sheds in the Division did a total of 12,320½ hours' work, which was divided as follows:—

Train Working		
Fast and Semi Fast Passenger	883¾	hrs.
Stopping Passenger	57¾	,,
Suburban Passenger	970¼	,,
Empty Stock (Main Line)	171¾	,,
Empty Stock (Suburban)	214¼	,,
Standing Time	1,016½	,,
PASSENGER TOTAL	3,314¼	,,
Parcels train	156¾	,,
Empty stock (parcels)	3¼	,,
PARCELS TOTAL	160	,,
Freight Trains (through)	390¾	,,
Pickup and feeder trains	302½	,,
Standing Time	53½	,,
FREIGHT TOTAL	746¾	,,
Departmental trains	26¾	,,
TRAIN WORKING TOTAL	4,247¾	,,
Shunting		
Passenger stock	654¼	hrs.
Parcels stock	74¾	,,
Freight (terminal)	429	,,
Freight (marshalling)	1¼	,,
Departmental stock	56½	,,
SHUNTING TOTAL	1,215¾	,,

Non-Revenue-Earning Activities

Acting as Conductor	53	hrs.
Working Light Engines	451	,,
Road Learning and Diesel Training	1,178	,,
Waiting Instructions	1,083	,,
Travelling	1,066¾	,,
Waiting for relief/to relieve	575½	,,
Physical needs/sickness	57½	,,
Preparation and disposal of Locos	479¼	,,
Shunting locos on shed	739¼	,,
Signing on and off	421½	,,
Attending meetings	45¾	,,
Reading Notices, Admin, etc.	706	,,
NON-REVENUE-EARNING TOTAL	6,857	,,
GRAND TOTAL	12,320½	,,

These figures, raw though they are, are instructive. It will be noticed above all that train working and shunting together accounted for less than half the total time spent; 44.3%, in fact. Now of course it is absurd to suppose that the whole of one's working day can be spent productively. One has to prepare oneself to do one's task, one has to train newcomers, and one has to put away one's tools. And yet; consider the figures. About 1,900 hours were spent actually driving passenger trains; to set against this there was empty stock working, standing time, and passenger shunting, amounting to rather more than 2,000 hours. Yet all this padding is still included as revenue-earning. What a lot of time is spent shuffling coaches about. It is quite surprising to find that in freight working, which one thinks of as involving lots of playing with wagons, train-running time was actually somewhat more than shunting time. Then again, look at the padding in the Non-Revenue-Earning list; working light engines, Road Learning and Diesel Training (what! nearly 10% of all time worked, with no new types being introduced and years after the end of steam?), shunting locos on shed, and above all Waiting for Instructions (i.e., "there's nothing for you today, mate; go and sit in the canteen"). Travelling looks pretty grotesque as well. The whole picture, which will be familiar to anyone who has ever wandered round a B.R. engine shed, is of far too many men employed with far too little to do. With a bit of organization and a necessarily brutal reduction of staff a reduction of 20-25% in hours worked to perform the same mileage and shunting ought to be achievable. This division was not untypical of the region as a whole except in having a larger proportion of rather better-organized suburban passenger and main-line work.

This does not, of course, mean that 20-25% of the regional footplatemen's wage bill could be saved, because of Mileage Payments. These form a very heavy addition to the wage packets of men on main-line work, and are a national all-time classic Bogus Productivity Scheme. Under the October 1965 Agreement a driver receives a minimum payment of 40 minutes' wages for any mileage run from nil to 65 (i.e., a minimum wage increase of 8%), and then extra bonus on an increasing taper so that, for example, he gets 2 hours' extra pay for running 125-132 miles, 2½ hours' pay for 140-147 miles, and thereafter an additional hour's pay for every additional 15 miles. At this rate the point is rapidly reached where all the benefit of any extra productivity goes in wage costs. It costs B.R. just as much to have one driver work a train from London to Newcastle as to have a change of crew halfway and both crews come home on the cushions: or if there is any saving it is more or less summed up by saying that the second crew then doesn't have to have a uniform or a pension. One can even save money in some cases by using two crews where one might serve. However, this is an extreme case. In the week's working analysis above, hourly pay came to £6,589, and mileage pay to £957, making a total payroll of £7,546.

But when every allowance is made, one ought still to be able to squeeze £3-4 million per annum out of the £20 million total of payments made to footplate staff alone in one region alone (and not the biggest region at that, so it wasn't the London Midland either). And management have never even tried. Maybe they fear the row, maybe they don't know how much juice can be squeezed out of this particular lemon. Neither reason reflects much credit. It's easier to close down branch lines or goods depots. How much was, say, the Aldeburgh branch losing when it got the chop? A four-figure sum. How much was the Somerset & Dorset losing? A six-figure sum. How much can be saved in this one isolated field on B.R. as a whole? A seven or eight-figure sum. What's management been doing? Grrrrr. Take a deep breath, go back and re-read prophecy No. 2, and see if you still disagree with it.

Of course, cutting costs is not really the best answer to the problem. So many of a railway's expenses are fixed and increase little if at all with extra traffic that the real way out of the maze is to increase revenue by increasing business. So there must be an end to the deliberate shedding of traffic before the prophecy can be falsified. But of course nothing excuses waste.

Prophecy No. 3. The Deficit will Increase

One might simply say Q.E.D. and leave it at that, but this would leave the Fairy Godmother out of the reckoning. One of the purposes of the Transport Bill (which may well be law by the time these words appear) is to relieve B.R. of the stigma of producing a colossal deficit; the 1969 accounts will be prepared on a different basis, with very large burdens in respect of capital debts and interest payments removed, and although the present global grant-in-aid to cover the deficit will also vanish there will be numerous individual subsidies (in respect of the provision of redundant facilities, continuation of moneylosing sundries and commuter services, etc.) which will appear as of right on the income side of the accounts. So on paper the 1969 deficit will certainly be less. But this will be the result of cooking the books.

No, it won't. It is very easy to cry "foul" when a player, because he cannot win the way the game is being played, changes the rules. But what if the rules really were unfair? There is a very powerful argument that this was so; that rail transport compared with road has been subjected to various crippling legal and accounting traditions and requirements, and that heavy road frieght transport in particular has never paid its proper costs. The Bill will remedy this position for the first time. Let us accept this case absolutely (although it would seem that in spite of coming to the rescue, possibly for the last time, Fairy Godmother does not in fact accept it). Charge withdrawn, therefore; and substituted "but this will be the result of a different presentation of the accounts." (*Charon: "It comes to the same thing!" Cerberus: growls and bites his leg*).

The other effect of the Transport Bill of course is alleged to be that it will divert a lot of freight back onto rail from road transport. I can't see this, myself; a system of road haulage licensing is to be set up, indeed, and permission to haul freight by road will be refused unless it can be shown that its transport wholly or partly by rail will be less advantageous to the customer in speed, reliability, and cost. But these are precisely the reasons why freight has been lost to road over the last twenty years. Any effect the Transport Bill will have on diverting freight back to the railways will therefore either be due to the built-in inertia of the licensing system, which puts most of the onus of proof on road (prophecy 3(b) is that we can look to the next Transport Bill, which will appear not later than 1972, to change this position); or because of the effect of the additional charges on road haulage proposed to be levied by the government. If the case for these charges is good, then they are legitimate, and we need not pay much attention to the road haulage propagandists who say that they impose a heavy new burden on the economy. Of course, the transport industry will meet a larger proportion of the total tax bill, but this is by no means the same thing. The government only wants to raise so much money in any year, so the burden will be correspondingly reduced elsewhere; it could even mean a few pence off income tax.

But there must be a limit to the amount of freight restored to rail, and it will be a strict limit, for two reasons: (i) the railways are no longer in the game for a very large, in fact overwhelming, proportion of the business; look at the closures of freight depots and removal of sidings all over the country. They're no longer physically able to handle a lot of the traffic they had even ten years ago. (ii) The Liner Train, being dependent on road shuttles at each end, will also be indirectly subjected to any new road charges or controls; and in an island this size the economy of the rail trunk haul cannot often be achieved over a long encugh distance to compensate for the delay and expense involved in having two road/rail transfer points on each journey. There is only a small place for the Liner Train; in that place it should, of course, be very profitable; but it will never in itself take much share in justifying a railway system.

The only way to redivert freight to rail, if this is what we want to do, is to say flatly "we're going to get as many lorries off the roads as possible, cost what it may" and then ban road haulage where rail can do the job (over, say, 40 miles). This is a viable policy; many countries do it. It ensures a healthy railway system and reasonably empty main roads. Prophecy 3(c) is that it won't be done in Britain in 1969. I didn't need the crystal ball for that one. But it could be done by 1979; it may have to be.

Prophecy No. 4. There will be no more main-line electrification

This is because electrification doesn't pay. This is partly because of the money that has been wasted on unnecessary frills in the past (and since the L.M.R. scheme, among others, is now complete, it is pointless as well as tedious and demoralizing to say how much more it cost than it need have); but it is mainly because, in Britain, electricity costs so much. In 1966 the total Eastern Region bill for diesel fuel was £1,267,000, to which a few thousand must be added for the cost of tanks, pumps, etc. The bill for the exact equivalent, electricity for traction purposes plus maintenance and amortization of overhead equipment, substations, etc., was £3,421,000. The only electrified lines, apart from one end of the Manchester-Sheffield scheme, were in the Liverpool Street suburban and outer suburban area. Electric freight train mileage was almost negligible. Electric passenger train mileage was slightly over 12 million; in passenger service alone diesel locomotives operated $10\frac{1}{2}$ million train miles, and diesel multiple-units $9\frac{1}{2}$ million. Freight was of course almost all diesel. The fuel costs of electric trains are therefore vastly higher than diesel; the savings of electrification are that locomotives, being simpler, are cheaper to buy and maintain. An L.M.R. electric locomotive costs about £8,700 per annum to have on the premises; a Type II diesel £8,000, and a Type IV diesel about £12,800. The electric is available for work 90% of the time while the diesel is available only 75% of the time; and the repair costs per mile are about 7d, 2/2d, and 3/- respectively. But this isn't enough to make electrification a worthwhile proposition; and the high cost of electricity means that dense traffic doesn't help to improve the case for electrification very much. In other countries it is different; other railways get their electricity cheaper. (Why? This needs another article).

The government has been aware of this for some time. Mr. Marples, it will be remembered, tried to stop the L.M.R. electrification. He found out the truth, and he was right to act in this way; but he was too late. Now we have the electrification, and of course it's splendid (so it should be). But there won't be any more, except possibly in suburban areas where other factors come into play.

The Ministry of Transport has in effect said politely to B.R.: "Excellent; you say electrification is a good thing. Very well then, you need not have our permission (although you will need the Treasury's): so go ahead and electrify. But find the money yourselves". Collapse of stout party. Very sad.

There is of course the argument that further electrification is essential for commercial reasons in order to ensure the future of the railway system. This is, of course, nonsense; it is all one to the customer whether trains are hauled by electric, diesel, steam, or clockwork locomotives, so long as the right service is offered at the right price. But if it were true, then it would mean the end of the railway system. Main-line electrification in Britain is as dead as that. The only thing that would resurrect it would be a complete government somersault on fuel policy, tipping the balance against imported fuels and so improving the economics of electric (and, for that matter, steam) traction. There would be a very good case for doing this, but it's not going to be done in the forseeable future. (Prophecy 4(b)). Sir Stanley Raymond's advocacy of really widespread electrification might even have had something to do with his abrupt departure from the B.R. chairmanship.

* * * * *

Were Dr. Lardner with us now, I have a feeling that public opinion would be better informed on transport policy than in fact it is. He has been much mocked for his arithmetical errors in the famous controversy with Brunel over Box Tunnel; we nevertheless lack a successor in his useful and neglected trade of Publiciser of Practical Science and Economics. Still, the issues are beginning to sort themselves out. B.R. have, during the last five or ten years, been savagely mauled by various outside experts professing various academic theories of what a railway should do and how it should be run; they have sometimes been aided and abetted by certain professionals who should have known better, but who were swept along by the current. Since it is easier to destroy than to build, the effect of all this has been mainly negative. The failure, except in a few commendable respects, is now becoming manifest. But the damage has been done. You will remember the spiel one still sometimes hears, about B.R. "getting down to a fighting weight". This has always conjured up in my mind the image of a desperately fat man reducing weight by having an arm or a leg amputated. Undeniably this is simpler and surer than dieting.

The Transport Bill (or Transport Act, 1968) is often said to have propped up the railways yet again. No, it hasn't. The truth of the matter is that the government have made up their minds that this is it; the question of whether the railway system is to survive is now open. The Bill falls over backwards to set B.R. on its feet for one last time: special subsidies for this, that, and everything imaginable, writing off of debts, the lot. The competition has also been somewhat hobbled. But the point of the whole structure of individual subsidies is that it can be dismantled piecemeal. The state no longer has the obligation to maintain a railway system. It has contracted out, left itself an escape route. There is no longer a single administrative obstacle to the step-by-step abolition of the network. If B.R. still runs deficits under the new set-up, the chopper will fall, and the whole darned lot will shut in fairly short order, leaving only the commuter lines. (And how long will they last? They may be essential to urban life as we know it, but there are plenty of things wrong with that; the city of 2069 may well have done away completely with the need to commute, and a good thing too).

B.R. have had the slate wiped clean. It is now up to them; and what will count is whether, after all the tribulations of ten unhappy years, they still believe in themselves. If they do, then nothing can stop them. If they don't, then nothing can save them. Put it another way: subsidies are no substitute for good management. They can always be withdrawn, and they will be, if it ever seems that the money is being wasted. Only good management can prevent waste.

Corris Railway 0–4–2T No. 3, built by the Falcon Engine Co. (a predecessor of English Electric) in 1878, in action on the Talyllyn near Abergynolwyn. [*J. B. Snell*

Private Railway Preservation in Britain

by R. C. Riley

My first encounter with railway preservation was in July 1951. I presented myself at Wharf Station, Towyn, paid my subscription to Tom Rolt, then General Manager of the Talyllyn Railway, and so became a member of the first project of its kind in this country. All was not well with the Talyllyn that day. The Corris 0–4–2T No. 3 "Sir Haydn" had made its second passenger-hauling journey that morning but had proved unsuited to the neglected state of the track. Running round the train at Abergnolwyn it had spread the road and derailed. The train crew managed to restore it to the rails and somehow a message was got down to Towyn to explain the delay. No through telephone communication then existed. I was conveyed through Towyn at a remarkable speed in Tom Rolt's vintage Alvis to assist John Snell in preparing *Dolgoch* at Pendre. However, John already had things under control, and as soon as No. 3 brought the train down the line, *Dolgoch* was ready to take over, so producing the then rare sight of two engines in steam at Wharf station.

Much has happened on the Talyllyn since those early days of Preservation Society ownership. Nearly 16,000 passengers were carried in 1951, a remarkable achievement bearing in mind that as Corris No. 3 had proved a broken reed the entire service was worked by the 1866 veteran *Dolgoch*, the only other engine in running order. What is more the only available stock consisted of four small coaches and two vans. The full story of the first two seasons of the Talyllyn has been told in Rolt's "Railway Adventure", one of the most readable railway books ever written.

Talyllyn history goes back to 1865, when slate traffic was first carried, passenger traffic commencing the following year. The two engines *Talyllyn* (1865) and *Dolgoch* (1866) provided the sole motive power to deal with the slate from Bryn Eglwys quarry that was the line's main business, together with such passenger traffic as there was. In 1946 the quarry closed and from then on the line had to rely entirely on summer tourists. The service had been suspended the previous year while *Dolgoch* was sent away for overhaul, since *Talyllyn* had been worked to a standstill. It was suspended again during the summer of 1949, while essential repairs were again carried out on *Dolgoch*. The railway owed its somewhat precarious existence to the interest of Sir Haydn Jones, who had acquired control in 1911, but on his death in the summer of 1950 it became abundantly clear that the railway, too, would perish at the end of that season unless something was done.

Hence the formation of the first Preservation Society to take over a railway, and happily from the outset its fortunes were guided by men of standing and experience, with boundless energy too. With only one engine in working order it was necessary to look elsewhere for additional motive power. Fortunately there was not far to look for the two Corris Railway engines survived at Machynlleth, having been out of use since flood damage closed the line in 1948. These were No. 3, Falcon Engine Co. of 1878 and No. 4 Kerr Stuart, 1921, both 0–4–2 saddle tanks, of which only the former had latterly been in running order. In 1954 a fourth steam engine arrived, an Andrew Barclay 0–4–0 tank of 1916 that had once seen service on a light railway, operated by the R.A.F. at Calshot, Hants. For track maintenance work, too, a small diesel proved an invaluable asset. Apart from the construction of new coaches, the rotting bodies of an old Corris Railway bogie and two diminutive Glyn Valley Tramway coaches have been magnificently restored. An interesting venture was the fitting of a Giesl Ejector to No 4. during 1959; comparative trials indicated a marked economy in coal consumption. The locomotive industry, notably the Hunslet Engine Company, has been very helpful to the Talyllyn; at one time or another all the engines have been extensively overhauled, and all except No. 6 completely reboilered. Apart from the operation of the line a narrow gauge museum has been established at Towyn and this is now run as a separate trust. The countless thousands of man hours that have been responsible for the tremendous success of the Talyllyn can never be computed; the vast outlay in L.S.D. can, because the Society has always published comprehensive accounts—they should be compulsory reading for any would-be preservation body. Looking to the future the Talyllyn plans a short extension of its $6\frac{1}{2}$ miles of track, now entirely relaid, but meanwhile it has much still to do in improving the present operational facilities. Measured in statistics, the success of the T.R.P.S. is shown by a membership over 2,500 and a record passenger complement during 1967 of nearly 109,000 single journeys.

During the first few weeks after revival in 1955 the Festiniog Railway only operated across the Traeth Mawr embankment at Portmadoc. In August of that year the veteran 0–4–0 "Prince" passes the entrance to Boston Lodge Works. [*J. B. Snell*

In 1951 during my stay at Towyn I also made my first acquaintance with its near neighbour, the Festiniog Railway. On arrival at Portmadoc I was directed to enquire for Mr. Robert Evans, Manager of the line, which had then lain derelict for five years. I found him at Boston Lodge Works and his initial reluctance to show me round was understandable when I saw what had been done by vandals who had broken in time and time again leaving destruction in their wake. All in all the railway was a sorry sight. The engines, rusty and neglected though they were, were under a reasonable degree of cover but carriages and wagons were rotting away in the open and parts of the track were spectacularly overgrown. It seemed a forlorn hope for preservation for although its 1 ft. 11$\frac{1}{2}$ in. gauge was less than the 2 ft. 3 in. of the Talyllyn its trackwork and rolling stock were heavier and larger.

The Festiniog Railway had been authorised by Act of Parliament as far back as 1832, and was opened throughout from Blaenau Festiniog to Portmadoc four years later. At first horses were responsible for haulage of the slate traffic that was the line's *raison d'etre*, but as this increased it became clear that some narrow gauge steam engines would have to be designed. The first of these arrived in 1863, four 0–4–0 tanks built in London at George England's works. Remarkably, three still survive, though only *Prince* is in serviceable condition. It was soon evident that these little engines, good as they were, did not have sufficient power to handle the increasingly heavy loads and an engineer named Fairlie designed a double four-coupled engine unit *Little Wonder* that proved more than twice as powerful as its predecessors. It was not an unqualified success and had a relatively short life, but it demonstrated, during 1870, the undoubted advantages of the design and the capacities of the narrow gauge to engineers from all over the world.

So on that sad visit in 1951 there were two "Double Fairlies" to be seen *Merddin Emrys* and *Taliesin*, built at Boston Lodge works in 1879 and 1885 respectively. *Taliesin* was in the erecting shop for retubing, the new tubes having been delivered before traffic ceased in 1946. Beside it was the 0–4–0 saddle tank *Prince*, frames and cylinders only, but with a brand new boiler ready to be fitted. Outside the works was a second 1863 engine, *Palmerston*, which had been supplying steam. On shed were seen *Princess*, another 1863 engine which had hauled the last train, *Welsh Pony*, a similar but larger engine of 1867 vintage, *Merddin Emrys* previously mentioned and the Welsh Highland Railway 1877 0–6–4 tank *Moel Tryfan*. This was a reminder of the nigger in the woodpile; for it was in its association with the insolvent Welsh Highland that the Festiniog lost thousands of pounds that it could ill afford. A journey on the Welsh Highland must have been an unforgettable experience, for it passed through very beautiful scenery, but in later years apart from a few summer tourists its traffic was negligible. Despite Festiniog help it closed in 1937; four years later the track was lifted and sold for scrap, as was one of the two surviving engines, a Baldwin 4–6–0 tank of 1917. The other, *Russell*, a Hunslet 2–6–2 tank of 1906 was sold for industrial service and has since been preserved. *Moel Tryfan* lingered on at Boston Lodge having been impounded by the Festiniog in 1936 against Welsh Highland debts. It was a doubtful asset and it so deteriorated in disuse that one of the first actions of the reformed Festiniog company in 1954 was to sell the remains for scrap. Robert Evans told me that there had been a public meeting in Portmadoc in 1950 when an attempt was made to get support for the preservation of the Festiniog Railway. He did not attend, considering the difficulties insurmountable.

At the time, walking through the derelict and forlorn shops and shed I was inclined to agree, but events were to prove me wrong for a Preservation Society was formed soon after, which set about trying to purchase shares in the company. Eventually Mr. A. F. Pegler became interested and he and others put up sufficient capital to obtain control of the railway. Unlike the Talyllyn, where the Society was directly responsible for the running of the railway and appointed a majority of directors of the Company which owned it, those who had put up the money

Welshpool & Llanfair No. 1 *The Earl* climbs over the hump between Cyfronydd and Heniarth with a train from Castle Caerienion to Llanfair on April 9, 1967. [Paul Riley

Taliesin coasting downhill through the forest between Plas and Cae Mawr. [*J. B. Snell*

The L & Y Pug No. 51218 on the third trip of the day crosses Healey Dell viaduct between Rochdale and Whitworth on a joint RVRS and LCGB Brakevan trip on 19th February 1967 [*J. G. Blears*

Britannia 4–6–2 No. 70004 *William Shakespeare* leaving Penrith in July, 1967 with a Carlisle-Birmingham express
[*J. M. Boyes*

Class 5 4–6–0 No. 44837 on a northbound freight crossing the motorway construction at Penrith in August 1967.
[*D. Cross*

Merchant Navy 4–6–2 No. 35007 *Aberdeen Commonwealth* on the down Bournemouth Belle at Pirbright; April 1967. This was the last regular top-class steam passenger working in Britain. [*J. B. Snell*

to buy the Festiniog elected to take control themselves. Nevertheless the Preservation Society has always been an effective supporters club and provider of additional finance, and from its ranks comes the volunteer labour that plays a large part in the operation of the line. There were gloomy forebodings that two preserved lines in the same area could not possibly succeed. These fears were groundless, since it is something of a Mecca for enthusiasts and indeed there is now a third preserved line not far away.

In July 1955 the Festiniog began a public service from Portmadoc to Boston Lodge, and in two months 20,000 passenger journeys were made. For the first few days a diesel tractor was used but then *Prince* took over and held the fort until nearly the end of the 1956 season, for which the line was cleared as far as Minffordd. That September *Taliesin* entered service again. The 1958 season saw trains running to Tan-y-Bwlch, and over 60,000 passengers were carried. This had been a tremendously exciting and stimulating period, but there was more to come. It was no longer possible to get through to Blaenau Ffestiniog over the old track because the Central Electricity Generating Board had constructed a reservoir that engulfed that part of the line by Moelwyn Tunnel, an appeal against this having been made in vain. Many would have been content to call it a day with 7½ miles of line operating. Not so the Festiniog—an elaborate plan was prepared for a deviation line, a Light Railway Order obtained, and work on the new line commenced in 1965. In 1968 the last remaining section of the old route below Moelwyn Tunnel, from Tan-y-Bwlch to the commencement of the new works at Dduallt, was opened: with a record 220,000 passengers and 4,500 society members in 1967, preservation of the Festiniog has been a real success story. Motive power is now provided by *Prince*, the two Double Fairlies, *Merddin Emrys* and *Earl of Merioneth* (formerly *Taliesin*), supplemented by two four-coupled saddle tanks from the Penrhyn Railway, *Linda* and *Blanche*, both of 1893 vintage. Boston Lodge also houses some privately preserved engines, the latest arrival being an Alco 1917 built 2–6–2 tank from the Tramway de Pithiviers à Toury, a sugar beet line closed at the end of 1964, and itself the subject of a French railway preservation venture: this engine has now been added to F.R. stock.

If much space has been devoted to the Talyllyn and Festiniog it is because their example paved the way for many further preservation efforts, not all of which have been so outstandingly successful. Preservation of a narrow gauge railway is one thing, that of the standard gauge quite another—the same problems, but on a larger scale, while negotiations with B.R. have often proved discouraging in the extreme. Nevertheless, at the time of writing there are two such lines operating and it is hoped that two more will have joined them during 1968.

A line with gradients of 1 in 30 and curves of 3½ chains radius in an industrial part of Leeds sounds an unpromising prospect but such was the first standard gauge line to be preserved. The Middleton Railway can proudly claim ancestry back to 1758 when parliamentary authority was given for the laying down of a "Waggonway" for the carriage of coals. What is more, steam traction was introduced to the 4½ mile line as early as 1812. After nationalisation of the coal industry the National Coal Board leased the line, decided that it worked at a loss and ceased to operate it, thereby leaving a number of firms with rail access but no trains. At the end of 1959 a number of enthusiasts from Leeds University decided to rectify this state of affairs and after much attention to the permanent way a portion of the line serving two works was reopened in the summer of 1960 and a regular freight service now operates exchanging traffic with B.R. to the extent of about 10,000 tons a year. The line is operated entirely by volunteers, motive power including a 150 h.p. 1932 vintage diesel purchased in June 1960 from its makers, Hunslet Engine Co., a small Fowler diesel, an 0–4–0 Sentinel steam locomotive built in 1933 for the L.N.E.R. and four industrial engines. On loan is a beautifully restored inside cylinder 0–4–0T built by the N.E.R. at Gateshead in 1891 and preserved in 1965 by the Steam Power Trust after a period of service

The Festiniog's 0–4–4–0 Double Fairlie "Taliesin" (now renamed "Earl of Merioneth") on the horseshoe curve below Tan-y-bwlch [*J. B. Snell*

Pride of the Scottish Railway Preservation Society is its Caledonian Railway 0–4–4T No. 419, now maintained at Falkirk. [*S.R.P.S.*

On the Bluebell Railway, ex-S.E. & C.R. 'P' class 0–6–0T No. 27 heads a train at Sheffield Park. The leading vehicle is an ex-London & North Western Observation Car. [*R. C. Riley*

Welshpool & Llanfair 0–6–0T No. 2 "The Countess" crossing the Banwy Bridge. [*A. J. Clarke*

with the N.C.B. The Middleton line has to be seen to be believed and is quite unlike any other preserved line anywhere but its job if not spectacular is worthwhile and carried on without fuss.

About the same time that the Middleton Railway scheme got under way attempts were being made to preserve another standard gauge line, that from Lewes to East Grinstead. Opened in 1882, the line closed in 1955, but owing to a legal anomaly had to be reopened in 1956; a token service worked until final closure two years later. When the line was closed there was considerable local opposition and Sussex newspapers referred to it as the Bluebell Line, a name that has stuck. Quite apart from the difficulties of operating 20 miles of line, the first three miles out of Lewes would have involved running over B.R. tracks still in use, as also was East Grinstead station. As a compromise the Bluebell Railway Preservation Society obtained a lease of the five miles of single line between Sheffield Park and Horsted Keynes, and reopened it in August 1960; although until the 1962 season its trains did not regularly enter Horsted Keynes station, instead using a halt platform outside.

Left: Possibly the most ambitious preservation scheme to get off the ground was the revival in 1967 of the 3′ 0″ gauge Isle of Man Railway, closed two years previously. 0–6–0T No. 15 "Caledonia" shunting at Douglas. [*G. W. Morrison* *Right:* The most active privately-owned locomotive to run on B.R., due to its owner's foresight in obtaining a contract, is Mr. A. F. Pegler's Gresley A3 Pacific "Flying Scotsman", now equipped with two tenders for extra water capacity. Here it heads a St. Pancras-Leicester special near Newton Harcourt. [*Brian Stephenson*

Since there was no run-round at the halt and trains could not be propelled, the entire rolling stock of two coaches and two engines, one at each end of the train, had to be used for every run that season, which up to the end of October brought the remarkable total of 15,000 passengers. The two engines were a L.B.S.C. "Terrier" 0–6–0 tank of 1875, restored to original livery in 1961 as No. 55 *Stepney*, and a similar S.E.C.R. engine, a P Class tank of 1910. The following year two more engines arrived, a second S.E.C.R. 0–6–0 tank and an 1885 Adams L.S.W.R. 4–4–2 tank, both of which were subsequently restored to their old company liveries. Also in 1961 four Metropolitan Railway coaches of 1900 vintage were acquired and this additional motive power and stock enabled 91,000 passengers to be carried in 1961. Since then further arrivals include G.W.R. No. 3217, a "Dukedog" 4–4–0, on loan having been preserved by an independent fund, and three engines purchased from B.R., a North London 0–6–0 tank of 1880, another Brighton "Terrier" of 1872, and an 1898 L.B.S.C. 0–6–2 tank. Further carriages purchased include a former L.N.W.R. Observation Saloon and the L.B.S.C.R. Directors Inspection Saloon.

No. 46201 "Princess Elizabeth" on display at Bath Road shed, Bristol, together with Dart Valley 0–6–0T No. 1638, in October 1967. Both locomotives came to Bristol under their own power.
[*Ivo Peters*

The Gresley Society's magnificently restored A4 "Sir Nigel Gresley" at the summit of Grayrigg Bank with a London-Carlisle special in April, 1967
[*Brian Stephenson*

Preserved "Castle" class 4–6–0 No. 7029 "Clun Castle" storms up Gresford Bank with a Birkenhead-Birmingham special in March, 1967.
[*John Goss*

Altogether, therefore, there is a formidable array of vintage rolling stock assembled at Sheffield Park and the line recorded 266,000 passenger journeys during 1967. All is not well with the Bluebell Railway, however, for unlike other operating societies it has not yet been able to purchase its line. In 1960 agreement was reached to pay B.R. a rent of about £2,250 per year, with an option to purchase at a cost of £34,000. When the five year agreement ended the rent increased to about £3,000 per year, since the line now included Horsted Keynes station, B.R. services there having been withdrawn in 1963. During 1968 the Bluebell Railway has to find the present purchase price of £43,500, of which it has taken three years to raise £20,000. Despite closeness to London and the South Coast towns, the Bluebell can only claim 1,100 members, or about one quarter of the membership of the Festiniog Society, in remote Wales. The Festiniog, of course is preserving history whereas the Bluebell has to make its own, and indeed can take pride in its achievements over a few years. Perhaps the Bluebell under-rates the value of its armchair members, those who pay a useful subscription but take no other part in society activities. At one time the "Bluebell News" was second to none among preservation society magazines, but now stringent economies make it a shadow of its former self and the Festiniog tops the league in this field. The latter society admits that cost of the magazine absorbs 25% of subscriptions but finds this worthwhile in terms of membership numbers. The journals published by the various societies and the A.R.P.S. "Railway Forum" play an important role in keeping distant members informed of developments. Whatever the cause of its flagging membership it is to be hoped that the Bluebell Railway will solve its difficulties and find the purchase price of its line, a visit to which can be a memorable experience.

The two standard gauge societies mentioned originated in 1959 and the apparent success of their efforts brought about a spate of preservation attempts. In this mania period all sorts of lines were mentioned as likely candidates ranging from the Somerset and Dorset and the Great Central London Extension to thoughts of revival of long defunct narrow gauge lines including the Southwold, Lynton and Barnstaple and Welsh Highland.

Nevertheless some sound preservation schemes did originate that year, including for example, the Railway Preservation Society, one of the prime movers in which was the late Noel Draycott. This Society conceived the idea of establishing depots where preserved stock could be maintained and once such collections had been built up thoughts would turn to the acquisition of a line. The three active districts of the R.P.S., namely London, West Midlands and Scotland, are now autonomous societies and have gone a long way in attaining their initial objective. In two depots north of London the London R.P.S. has a Beattie L.S.W.R. 2–4–0 tank of 1874, a Metropolitan Railway 0–4–4 tank of 1898, some industrial engines and various items of stock including vintage G.N., L.N.W.R. and L.C.D.R. coaches. The West Midlands R.P.S. has a depot at Hednesford, where its relics include a L.B.S.C.R. 0–6–0 tank of 1877, industrial engines, a North Western T.P.O. vehicle, a Midland Royal Saloon, a Maryport & Carlisle Railway four-wheeled coach and other items of passenger and freight rolling stock. Considerable activity is now directed on a former N.C.B. line at Chasewater, Staffs., where a new depot is to be built and the stock will be seen at work. The Scottish Society, too, has amassed a considerable amount of interesting rolling stock at its Falkirk depot, but is especially proud of its beautifully restored 1907 Caledonian Railway 0–4–4 tank. It also owns an 1891 North British 0–6–0 and an industrial 0–4–0 well tank built at Leith in 1861, together with some passenger and freight stock.

First launched in 1959, too, was the M. & G.N. Joint Railway Society which planned to preserve the line from North Walsham Town to Yarmouth Beach. This ambitious scheme came to nothing and thoughts were then turned to the Melton Constable—Norwich City line. This, too, did not materialise and the

Time was when B.R. themselves were better appreciative of the money-making possibilities of operating preserved steam power especially in Scotland. In May, 1962, the Caledonian's 4–2–2 No. 123 and North British 'Glen' 4–4–0 No. 256 headed a special returning to Glasgow up the 1 in 50 out of Oban.
[*C. Lawson Kerr*

present plan is to acquire the line from Sheringham to Weybourne. The Society now uses both stations and at the former has a Great Eastern 0–6–0 of 1912, one of the once ubiquitous J.15's first built in 1883, and a L.N.E.R. built 4–6–0, a Gresley B.12/3 rebuild of Great Eastern design. It also owns two diesel railbuses and a four coach set of Gresley articulated suburban coaches.

Another 1959 venture has met with resounding success. The Ravenglass & Eskdale Railway started life in 1875 as a 3 ft. gauge line to carry iron ore traffic and survived in this form until 1912. It was resuscitated as a 15 in. gauge line between 1915 and 1917 and carried much freight and passenger traffic. It eventually came into the ownership of the Keswick Granite Company, whose quarries on the line closed in 1953. This Company advertised the railway for sale as a going concern in 1958 and it was sold by auction two years later to the Preservation Society, thanks largely to the financial assistance of Mr. Colin Gilbert, now Chairman of the new operating company. The railway was in reasonably good condition and apart from internal combustion engines it owned two steam locomotives, the 2–8–2 *River Esk* of 1923 and the 0–8–2 *River Irt* of 1928. The line is seven miles long and traverses some very pleasant countryside on the fringe of the Lake District. Thanks to considerable publicity and a strong membership it goes from strength to strength. Its passenger journeys of 185,000 in 1967 make an impressive total for a 15 in. gauge line, but even this is overshadowed by another remarkable achievement. In December 1966 the railway took delivery of a brand new steam locomotive, the 2–8–2 *River Mite*. Built at York, it was ordered on the strength of the progress of the Society's appeal to raise £7,500 for the purpose. No less an achievement was that it was transported to Ravenglass over the Pennines in appalling weather conditions behind a steam traction engine! Once having overcome initial teething troubles *River Mite* has settled down to being a useful member of the R. & E.R. stud and for engines in immaculate condition these three take a lot of beating.

At the same time that work was going on to preserve the Ravenglass & Eskdale another society was formed to take over the 2 ft. 6 in. gauge Welshpool & Llanfair line. From the outset in 1903 the Welshpool & Llanfair was closely associated with the Cambrian Railways and when the latter company was merged into the G.W.R. on 1 January 1922 it was clear that the independent days of the narrow gauge line were numbered. It too was absorbed a year later and in 1931 passenger traffic was withdrawn. When, in 1956, freight traffic finished and the line closed there were immediate thoughts of preservation, bearing in mind the ever increasing traffic receipts of the other two Welsh preserved lines. A

Preservation Society was formed and after lengthy negotiations with B.R. permission was obtained to start clearance work on the line. The following year the Society was wound up and a Preservation Company formed, limited by guarantee. In July 1961 *The Earl*, one of the line's two Beyer Peacock 0–6–0Ts returned after five years absence in store at Oswestry, and in October 1962 *Countess*, the second engine joined it. Four miles of the line from Llanfair to Castle Caereinion was reopened in April 1963, extended by 1¼ miles to Sylfaen the next year, when unfortunately the bridge over the River Banwy was badly damaged by floods. With the help of the Royal Engineers the bridge was repaired and this serious setback overcome. Apart from the two original engines, the line owns two diesels, an unusual Sentinel steam engine from the London Brick Company and *Monarch* a 1953 built Bagnall articulated locomotive from Bowater Lloyds, Sittingbourne. The passenger coaches came from the Chattenden and Upnor Railway, owned by the Admiralty. In 1967 the Welshpool & Llanfair recorded that 22,461 single journeys were booked, substantially less than the other Welsh preserved lines and only about a quarter of the passengers carried on the Vale of Rheidol, V.R.'s surviving Welsh narrow gauge line, which is not particularly well advertised.

One final event in 1959 took place when Captain W. G. Smith purchased from B.R. a G.N.R. Ivatt 0–6–0 saddle tank of 1897, so becoming the first person in this country to buy a standard gauge engine. Beautifully restored in G.N. livery, and in full working order, the engine is at present in Yorkshire.

In 1960 the British Transport Commission published its list of 71 steam locomotives already preserved or earmarked for preservation. Inevitably this ambitious list could not cater for all tastes and there was a spate of letters to the railway press deploring the fact that this, that and the other engine had been omitted from the official collection. One such letter to RAILWAY WORLD is worth recalling. Its writer, one R. Bell, regretted the failure to preserve L.N.E.R. 4–6–2

One of the hazards of private locomotive ownership is the attention of thieves; nameplates, especially, must be stored in safe custody, and refitted before each run. [*Ian C. Gumm*

On the other hand, there are willing helpers to lend a hand with cleaning, as here to Lord Garnock's Gresley K4 2–6–0 "The Great Marquess", at Nine Elms. [*G. R. Hounsel*

Flying Scotsman, L.M.S. 4–6–0 *Royal Scot* and L.M.S. 4–6–2 *Princess Elizabeth*. As it turned out *Flying Scotsman* was bought privately by Mr. A. F. Pegler in 1963, *Royal Scot* went to Butlin's Skegness holiday camp the same year and *Princess Elizabeth* on withdrawal in 1962 became the subject of a preservation appeal by the above mentioned R. Bell. To save such a large locomotive by individual donations seemed an enormous task but it says much for Roger Bell's tenacity of purpose that the Princess Elizabeth Locomotive Society secured not only the locomotive itself but now has two L.M.S. corridor coaches to go with it. *Princess Elizabeth* arrived at its new home at Ashchurch in August 1963. Buying a large locomotive is one thing but keeping it in good condition when stored in the open is quite another. Thanks to hard work by a few dedicated members this had been achieved, and two years after arrival at Ashchurch came the long awaited day when it was steamed for the first time. Fortunately a thrush that had nested under the footplate had raised its brood and flown away! Much had been done, including the fitting of a new brick arch in the firebox. When water was put in the tender for the first time leaks were so bad that it had to be emptied, causing flooding of the track, which sagged under the weight. Roger Bell managed to fit new asbestos gaskets and in the process everything was damped but his enthusiasm! It was all right on the day although there were some anxious moments when it was found easy to move the engine on a short siding, less easy to stop it. Much has been learnt since then and in 1967 *Princess Elizabeth* steamed to and from Bristol at the invitation of B.R. for Open Day at Bath Road depot.

The Ashchurch site mentioned is part of a unique preservation venture, for it is a private siding at one of the works of the Dowty Group. This enlightened firm runs an active Sports and Social Club and railway preservation has become one section, along with cricket, tennis, and so on. The Dowty Railway Preservation Society owns the only surviving vehicle of the G.W.R. 1935 Centenary stock, a restaurant car. There is also a G.W.R. saloon of 1881 and an Avonside 0–4–0 tank donated by Cadbury Bros. among smaller and no less interesting relics.

For preservation of G.W. relics the palm must surely go to the Great Western Society, established in 1962. Now, either the Society or individual members own no less than seven locomotives, a diesel railcar, ten coaches and a goods brake van. Largest items are the 4–6–0's *Burton Agnes Hall* at Didcot and *Cookham Manor* at Ashchurch. Didcot also houses a 2–6–2 tank and an 0–4–2 tank, Ashchurch an 0–6–2 tank and there is an 0–6–0 saddle tank at Totnes. The relatively modern engine shed at Didcot is an ideal place for much of the stock to be safely housed, being far removed from public access. During 1968 the Society planned three Open Days when trains would operate on the short branch from Cholsey to Wallingford. The Society's progress is indeed a tribute to the enthusiasm of lovers of the G.W.R.

At the same time that the Great Western Society was established initial moves took place to form the Dart Valley Railway Preservation Society to buy and operate the attractive 9½ mile branch from Totnes to Ashburton. This in the event, turned out to be a different venture because several business men teamed together with the hope of running the line at a profit, while the Preservation Society acts as a supporters club on Festiniog lines. This, too, has been successful in preserving a considerable amount of G.W.R. stock and it has 8 tank locomotives and 14 coaches at Buckfastleigh, the depot of the line. In 1968 it hoped to start operating trains between Staverton and Buckfastleigh. The future of the line thence to Ashburton is obscure pending a decision as to improvements of the A.38 trunk road. Nevertheless the line in its present form is worth visiting and most of the stock has been restored to G.W.R. livery.

Another society hoping to reopen part of a G.W.R. branch is the Severn Valley Railway Society, with a depot at Bridgnorth, aiming to run 4½ miles to

Hampton Loade. It has a G.W.R. 0–6–0 and a diesel car saved by G.W. Society members, an L.M.S. Class "2" 2–6–0 built by B.R. in 1950, the last Manning Wardle engine ever built, an 0–6–0 saddle tank of 1926 preserved by the Warwickshire Railway Society, and an ex Port Talbot Railway 0–6–0 tank bought from the N.C.B., the subject of a private preservation fund. Stock at Bridgnorth also includes six G.W.R. coaches and a milk van. The Society has a long way to go in raising funds to buy the line but is working hard to this end. There is some uncertainty as to the route of a by-pass road at Bridgnorth but it is hoped that this difficulty can be overcome.

The last two schemes mentioned face difficulties from new road works and the same difficulty killed one promising preservation scheme, that of the 4¾ mile branch from Dunton Green to Westerham. After much restoration work had been done Kent County Council bought the line as part of a new ring road and disappointed supporters threw in their lot with the Kent & East Sussex Railway Preservation Society.

Although formed as far back as 1961, the K. & E.S.R. Society has had perhaps more than its fair share of setbacks. The 13½ mile line from Robertsbridge to Tenterden was one of a group of independent light railways run by Colonel H. F. Stephens. The portion remaining was opened throughout by 1902 and taken over by B.R. in 1948. The passenger service was withdrawn in 1954 and freight traffic ceased seven years later. It was a delightful line through attractive countryside but as a preservation prospect seemed beset with difficulties. It crosses some marshland and has in the past been flooded, involving increased costs of maintenance. Its several bridges will only carry locomotives of very light axle load and there are no less than eight level crossings, of which four are over main trunk roads. Despite hard work on the track by society members, installation of a replacement telephone system throughout the line and the assembly of a large amount of locomotives and rolling stock the future looks bleak for the K.E.S.R., its application for a Light Railway Order having been rejected by the Minister of Transport. To overcome this it has resorted to litigation, a process which is always costly and seldom successful when directed against a government department. The outcome is not known at the time of writing. Meanwhile at Robertsbridge stands a restored S.E.C.R. 0–4–4 tank of 1905, owned by a Trust and originally intended for use on the Westerham line. Another engine on loan is a Brighton Terrier of 1876, while the Society has bought an 1872 member of the same class originally sold to the K.E.S.R. (then the Rother Valley Railway) in 1901. There are also eight industrial locomotives, a G.W.R. diesel railcar, five coaches and two Pullman cars.

A more promising project seems to be that of the Keighley & Worth Valley Railway Preservation Society, to revive the 4¾ mile Midland Railway line from Keighley to Oxenhope closed in 1962. After lengthy negotiations and much hard work on track, buildings and stock the plan may materialise in 1968, a hire purchase agreement having been entered into with B.R. The Society has assembled at Haworth the largest collection of privately owned locomotives and coaches in the country, mostly owned by private individuals or preservation fund raising bodies. Among those in the former category are "Royal Scot" 4–6–0 *Scots Guardsman*, an L.M.S. type Class "2" 2–6–2 tank and a N.E.R. type 0–6–0 tank both built by B.R., Captain Smith's G.N.R. saddle tank, an 1887 L. & Y.R. 0–6–0 and an American-built 0–6–0T used by the S.R. on Southampton Docks. Those saved by various funds include two L. & Y. 0–4–0 "Pug Tanks" and an 1881 0–6–0 saddle tank, property of the L. & Y. Saddletanks Fund, the Gresley Society's 1921 G.N. 0–6–2 tank and the Midland 1F Fund's Johnson 0–6–0 tank of 1880. Latest acquisition is a 1926 L.M.S. "Crab" 2–6–0 loaned by the B.R. Custodian of Historical Relics. Five industrial engines and a diesel bring the stock total to 18, while there are two diesel railbuses, two Pullman cars, ten bogie and three non-bogie coaches. The line has steep gradients to negotiate leaving Keighley

Left: The Gresley Society's N2 class 0–6–2T No. 4744 at Oxenhope on a special working over the Keighley & Worth Valley line in 1965. [*Ian G. Holt* *Right:* At Bridgnorth on the Severn Valley line: Collett 0–6–0 No. 3205 on a special working in 1967. [*John R. Hillier*

but passes through pleasant scenery at the country end and Haworth in the heart of the Brontë country is already a tourist centre.

Another society recently formed in Yorkshire has the object of operating the attractive 18 mile line from Pickering to Grosmont. Although it has considerable local support negotiations have not yet reached an advanced stage and considerable funds must be raised to purchase the line and provide motive power and stock.

It has been impossible within the framework of this article to mention every preservation scheme for it is a remarkable fact that including the national collection there are over 400 locomotives preserved in this country. Some have already been mentioned and others include the L.N.E.R. 4–6–2 *Sir Nigel Gresley* (Gresley Society), L.M.S. 4–6–0 *Bahamas* (Stockport Locomotive Society) S.R. 4–6–2's *Clan Line* (Merchant Navy P.S.) and *Blackmore Vale* (Bulleid Locomotive P.S.) an S.E.C.R. 0–6–0 of 1902 (Wainwright P.S.), a North Eastern Railway 0–6–0 of 1923 and an 0–8–0 of 1918 (North Eastern Loco. Preservation Group), an L.N.W.R. 0–6–2 Coal Tank of 1888 now looked after by the National Trust at Penrhyn Castle, and a Caledonian 0–6–0 of 1899 (Scottish Loco. Preservation Fund), the latter now being in the Glasgow Transport Museum. Quite apart from these there are many engines owned by private individuals ranging from Gresley Pacifics and G.W. "Castles" to narrow gauge industrials, of which noteworthy examples are the Bagnall saddle tank *Pixie* at Cadeby Rectory, Leicestershire and some varied types at Bressingham Hall, Norfolk.

Until comparatively recently there was little or no co-ordination between the various preservation societies. Now happily, the picture is very different, since the Association of Railway Preservation Societies is becoming well established under the able guidance of its Chairman, Captain Peter Manisty, R.N., backed by a well qualified team. The B.R. Scrap Sales Controller found the A.R.P.S. of invaluable guidance in sorting the wheat from the chaff among the fantastically large number of enquiries received from would be locomotive buyers, and more recently the B.R. Custodian of Historical Relics has agreed that some items stored on his behalf should go to A.R.P.S. member societies. The Association is represented on the Consultative Panel for the Preservation of British Transport Relics and recently it negotiated with the Army Department for three engines belonging to member societies to find a home on the Longmoor Military Railway. It has approved an exhaustive Code of Practice for member societies and voting powers will be restricted to those who conform. Already it has over 50 full or observer members, including most of the societies mentioned above. There are some curious omissions, including the Talyllyn, which claimed at its 1967 A.G.M. that as the pioneer body it needs no help and would get nothing out of A.R.P.S. membership. Fortunately the other pioneer body, the Festiniog, takes the wider view and is an active member, being happy to let the A.R.P.S. as a whole benefit from its expertise and experience.

Whether within the A.R.P.S. or not, the future of private railway preservation seems assured and one looks forward in the next decade to a consolidation of the considerable progress made in the last decade.

Railway Preservation on the Continent

by J. H. Price

When the scheduled steam-hauled passenger train in North America became extinct, some 12-15 years ago, it began to dawn on interested parties that a steam train was now something that people would come a long way to see and travel in, and something which, properly handled, could make money for its promoters. Gradually, a new kind of railway came into being, the commercial or educational steam-tourist railroad, of which North America now has some three dozen.

In recent years, it has been fascinating to apply the same logic to Europe, and to try and pinpoint the likely emergence of steam-tourist lines on this side of the Atlantic. Several European countries are now virtually steamless—Britain, Ireland, Holland, Switzerland, Denmark, Belgium, Sweden—and others will follow. In each there is scope for a steam-tourist revival, and after a late start, Europe is rapidly catching up with North America.

The first such lines in Europe were in Britain. On the Continent, the honours were shared between France and Denmark. At Meyzieu, nine miles east of Lyons, a group of enthusiasts headed by J. Arrivetz started in 1959 to build a new 60 cm. gauge light railway on which to run a little train recalling those that once could be found all over France. Regular service began in 1962, and at summer weekends the Chemin de fer Touristique de Meyzieu does quite good business, with a season extending from Easter to the end of October. Soon, a brand new track is to be built on a separate location,

In the same year, 1962, the Danish Railway Club came to an arrangement with the private Lolland Railway to use the standard-gauge branch from Maribo to Bandholm for a museum train. Since the Lolland Railway use the line on weekdays for freight, the museum train can only run on Sundays, but it draws crowds from all over Denmark, and (since it is quite near Rodby, with its ferry from Puttgarden) also from Germany. Most trains are steam-hauled, but there is also a vintage petrol railcar. Maribo-Bandholm set a useful precedent in

Left: C de F Touristique de Meyzieu's 0–8–0T "Bourgogne", one of the many identical machines built for service behind the German lines in the 1914-18 war. [*M. Geiger* *Right:* One of the 2–6–2Ts on the 75-cm gauge Sorumsand line, in Norway. [*A/L Hløandsbanen*

getting its services shown in the State Railways timetable, in antique Gothic fount. The gem of its fleet is a 2–4–0 tender engine complete with cowcatcher.

In Sweden, steam tourist activity began in the same way as in France; enthusiasts bought up some 60 cm. gauge locomotives and rolling stock, and set about looking for somewhere to run them. After a false start, the Swedish Railway Club took over a brickworks line at Mariefred, about 30 miles south-west of Stockholm, and christened it the Ostra-Södermanlands Järnväg. It runs on Sundays from mid-May to the end of September, about every 35-45 minutes, and is operated very professionally, with uniformed staff, printed timetables and a train departure indicator. If you go there by train, alight at Läggesta.

The most heartening story is that of Norway, where despite the low population density, no fewer than three steam-tourist lines exist, all of narrow gauge. The Norwegian Railway Museum at Hamar (run by the State Railways) has a 75-cm. gauge track on which a locomotive and carriage sometimes run, and the line from which they came (the Aurskog-Høland line) itself survives in part, with a steam tourist service on Sundays from June to September. This railway is about 20 miles east of Oslo, at Sørumsand, and is known today as the Tertitten Railway. The trains are worked by two 2–6–2 tank engines, and the society (A/L Hølandsbanen) publishes leaflets in English as well as Norwegian. The third museum line is the Grovane-Beihølen section of the 1,067 mm. gauge Byglandsfjord railway, north of Kristiansand, and here again it is fascinating to read how the Norwegian State Railways readily agreed to leave the track down after closure and lease it at a nominal rent, with engines and stock, to the local enthusiasts. They even laid on a driving instructor!

Before we leave Scandinavia, one more line must be mentioned, this time brand new. Early in 1967, the Swedish State Railways closed the last 24 miles of their 891 mm. gauge line into Gothenburg and cut the trains back to Sjøvik (with a bus connection into town), to free the land for other use. The railfans of Gothenburg, not wishing to be outdistanced by their opposite numbers in Stockholm, have arranged to lease part of the disused line at Sjøvik and run a steam passenger service at summer weekends, and since 891 mm. gauge was used widely in Sweden, sometimes for really long lines, they will be running a much more imposing train than most, with a tender engine and gaslit bogie coaches.

In Belgium, the enthusiasts are kept busy staffing the splendid tramway museum created by the SNCV at Schepdaal, about eight miles west of Brussels on the road to Ninove. It contains three static steam tram engines, but efforts to lay a working track nearby came to naught. Instead, in 1964, they were given a lease of a 9.4 km. metre-gauge line from Erezée to Dochamps in the Ardennes, once forming part of the long Vicinal line from Manhay to Melreux, which was built as a steam tramway but was later worked by diesel *autorails*. Its new name is the *Tramway Touristique de l'Aisne* (TTA), and since July 1966 it has run a public service with diesel cars and open and closed trailers on Tuesday and Sunday afternoons in mid-summer, the operating season growing slightly longer each year. The long-term aim is to use steam, in the form of a genuine Vicinal tram engine, but since the only ones available need heavy repairs, the first steam locomotive on the line will be a non-tramway engine recently purchased in France.

In 1966, France acquired a second steam-tourist line, again on the 60 cm. gauge, 58 miles south of Paris. This is part of the former *Tramway de Pithiviers à Toury*, a roadside line which ran a public service until 1951 and handled sugar-beet each autumn until closure in 1965. The TPT had quite a large stock of engines (of which two went after closure to Meyzieu, and one to Britain), but there were no passenger coaches, and the lessee society has had to build its own (some rebuilt from Valenciennes trams). The train, usually steam but sometimes a veteran railcar, runs on Sunday afternoons from mid-April to mid-October, and there are plenty of museum items to see in the big depot at Pithiviers.

France also has three seaside pleasure lines of the same gauge, at Arcachon, St. Trojan and Merlimont-Plage, but only the third uses steam; the second has an engine, but fire risk in the woods prevents its use. The Merlimont line is not far from Le Touquet, and can easily be visited on a day trip from Britain; it was built in 1967. These three lines run every day, but only at the height of the season, July and August.

In Germany, organised railway-enthusiasm was a late starter, and until five or six years ago there were few magazines or clubs, and no sign of museum activity. Since then, the Germans have caught up rapidly, and today they have a delightful metre-gauge railway at Bruchhausen-Vilsen, south of Bremen, operated by the *Deutsche Kleinbahn-Verein* on tracks leased from the Hoya-Syke-Asendorf railway. Up to now, it has only run on alternate Sunday afternoons from mid-May to late August (the dates are in the German Railways' timetable), but 1969 should see more operating days, and plans are afoot for a similar line in the south, possibly by a lease of the Jagsttalbahn from Mockmühl to Dörzbach.

The most recent country to join the operating list is Switzerland. With light railways all around them, and a superb professional transport museum at Lucerne, Swiss enthusiasts did not feel the same need to start their own museum railway, but the attraction of steam is fully recognised now, and the idea has the backing of the tourist authorities, who in Switzerland count for quite a lot. The line chosen for steam-tourist operation is the Chamby-Blonay branch of the metre-gauge *Chemins de fer Veveysans* above Montreux, leased to a *Comité d'Initiative* of enthusiasts, most of whom are professional transport men doing it in their spare time. They can also run electric trains, but have three steam locomotives including a Mallet (No. 104) from the Zell-Todtnau line in Germany, which should be able to manage the gradients, though I am not so sure about the two 0–6–0 tanks. Operation was due to start in June or July 1968, and to hear a steam engine blasting up from Blonay (2,043 ft.) to Chamby (2,465 ft.) will be well worth the trip.

Lastly, 1969 will see the start of steam-tourist operations in Holland, this time standard-gauge. The Dutch *Tramweg-Stichting* has a collection of some 80 vehicles, many of them from the 3 ft. 6 in. gauge RTM tramway that closed in 1966; these are stored at Hellevoetsluis, but a lease is being taken of the Netherlands Railways branch from Hoorn to Medemblik, north of Amsterdam, and here the T.S. will run a passenger train at weekends with a Henschel tram engine of 1921 (ex-Gooische Tramweg) and two tank-engines from Rotterdam gasworks.

What other countries are there? In Spain, Portugal and Italy, enthusiasts are too thin on the ground to make a museum line practicable, though there are a few individually-owned relics. The Austrians have the Zillertalbahn, as good as any Welsh line, but it would not be surprising to see a steam-tourist line come into being somewhere around Vienna. As for Eastern Europe, the Pioneer Railways (worked by children) are akin to our own miniature railways, and some still use steam, notably the 15-inch gauge lines at Leipzig and Dresden. Most, however, have never known steam at all, for they were built to teach children how to run railways as a career, and by the time they grow up, the railways will be diesel or electric.

All the steam-tourist lines have one main feature in common; they use small, economical engines of light railway or industrial types, pulling one, two or three coaches. They are great fun to ride, but when steam traction has disappeared from Europe's main lines, they will hardly give future generations of schoolchildren a true idea of what a real main-line steam train was like. Once again, Britain is leading the way (in-Europe) with the private preservation of some really large main-line engines; a few have been kept in Switzerland (including a Pacific from Bavaria and another from France), but there is room for several more standard-gauge steam-tourist lines in Europe to show how we used to travel. Will this be the pattern of the next few years? I hope so.

Rebuilding and upgrading B.R. Diesel Locomotives

by Dr. (Dipl. Ing.) A.E. von Dampf

In the decade from 1958 to 1968, British Railways placed in service approximately 4,500 diesel locomotives, mostly with electric, but including some with hydraulic, transmission. Many of these performed satisfactorily in shunting duty, but of those designed for main line work considerable anxiety has been felt as they have not come up to expectations either in respect of performance or of reliability.

The situation was reached where adverse comment was made both in Parliament and in the Press. To remedy the situation, Dr. von Dampf of the Advanced Research Department, Derby, was given the task of developing a design to meet all foreseeable conditions in the most economical way. This bulletin summarises the results.

I—Troubles with Existing Locomotives

The high rate of dieselization embarked upon by British Railways from 1956 brought with it many headaches, including "teething troubles" which failed to dissipate, resulting in chronic unreliability. Power outputs in many instances were inferior to the former steam locomotives which had been replaced.

Unreliability manifested itself not only within the diesel engines themselves, but in the control gear, the electric transmission in the case of diesel-electric, and the cardan shafts in the case of diesel hydraulic, locomotives; whilst many auxiliaries, in addition to absorbing much of the output from the crankshaft, gave grave cause for anxiety. Steam heating, for example, with its attendant auxiliary boilers, was a source of recurrent failure of the most widely publicized variety.

A further disadvantage encountered was that of the crew falling asleep on duty, largely due to the monotony of driving these machines for long periods under peculiarly uninteresting conditions.

II—Remedies

The first, and obvious, improvement sought was the building of new diesels of greater power, 4,000 h.p. being considered desirable by the Operating Department. However, investigation showed that this required a great deal of capital investment in the development of the required high-power engines; and whilst the desired output could be attained readily enough in laboratory trials there could be no assurance of the improved reliability also sought. Furthermore, as pointed out by the accountants, many of the existing diesels were comparatively new, and it was considered undesirable to write them off entirely when numerous basic components were still capable of further service.

Accordingly, the alternative policy of rebuilding and upgrading was decided on, and by means of bold and unconventional principles of design it was found feasible to develop a scheme for uprating an existing diesel of 1,500 h.p. to 5,000 h.p. at only one third of the cost of a new locomotive of equivalent power, whilst at the same time so simplifying the machinery that the utmost reliability could be positively guaranteed. The principles of the conversion will now be described.

Firstly, the conventional diesel engine is discarded and its place as the prime source of power taken by a new unit, which is coupled to the old to form a twin-unit locomotive. This new unit comprises basically a reactor in which fuel, solid or liquid as desired, is transformed chemically to an active gaseous state. This process takes place at a high temperature in a fluid-cooled chamber. The gases then pass through a heat-exchanger, and in doing so transfer their heat to the Transmission Fluid, which normally attains 325 °F at which point it vaporises. Part of the gases are then used to reheat the Transmission Fluid in its vaporised condition to a temperature falling in the range of 550-775 °F whereupon it is ready for use. The efficiency of the reactor and heat-exchanger, which are integrally combined within a single structure, varies with output, but is always high, ranging from 60% to 85%.

Having been heated to the required temperature, the Transmission Fluid is led to a simple but ingenious heat engine (comprising two cylinders only) where it is converted into mechanical energy. Such is the flexibility and effectiveness of this engine, that the normal electrical or hydro-mechanical transmissions are eliminated entirely, and the power taken directly to the wheels. Once again, the mechanical efficiency of this system is high, being of the order of 80-85%.

An interesting inherent phenomenon of this system, observed during the course of trials, is a consequence of the fact that a comparatively large volume of Transmission Fluid is always present in the heat-exchanger. This forms a useful reservoir of stored energy which, by depletion, enables the locomotive to produce for limited periods of several minutes at a time, power outputs as much as 50% above the continuous rating. The advantage in this respect over conventional locomotives is important.

Control equipment is of an extremely simple nature, and is housed in a single cab at the rear of the leading unit. Apart from the suppression of the usual second cab, arrangements for multiple-unit operation can be dispensed with at a worth-while capital saving, for the locomotive is of sufficient power as to obviate the need for such operation.

Auxiliaries necessary for the successful functioning of the locomotive are what would till now have been considered impossibly few. The demand for train heating is met on the prototype by retaining the original auxiliary generator, but an important modification whereby the train would be heated directly by a supply of vaporised transmission fluid is under urgent study.

III—Broader Implications of the Rebuilding

One useful characteristic of this locomotive may prove to be its ability to burn a variety of fuels, which in view of the current attitudes of the Afro-Asian Powers, will be of great interest. Ample supplies of indigenous fossil fuel are available. This fuel, together with a reserve of Transmission Fluid, is stored in the body of the rear unit in the space made available by removal of engines, generators, etc.

A further economy to be gained from these locomotives arises from their general ruggedness of construction which enables them to perform reliably without the expensive and elaborate terminals and highly skilled technicians at present necessarily employed in them under highly unhealthy and unattractive conditions of heavy pollution by diesel fumes, etc.

IV—Future Policy

Following the success of the first prototypes, British Rail are planning a large programme of rebuilding, with a view to converting and upgrading all existing locomotives on the above principles as rapidly as their workshop is able.

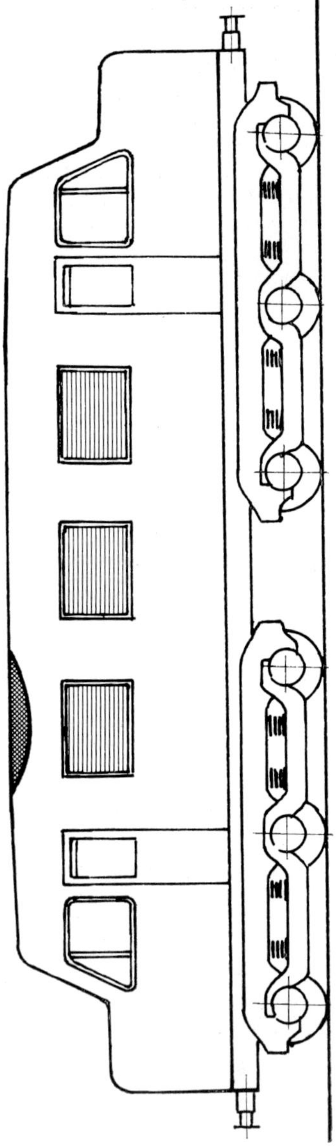

DIESEL BEFORE CONVERSION (1500 HP)

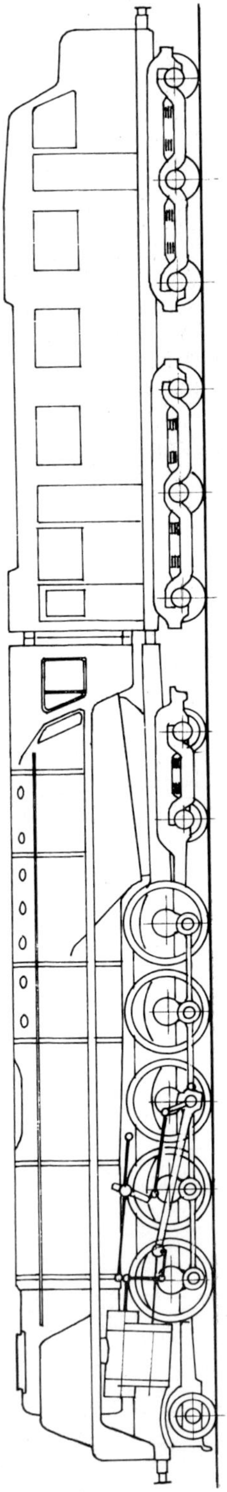

DIESEL AFTER CONVERSION (4000/5000 HP)

The Nice-Paris "Cote-d'Azur Express" at Monte Carlo in 1905, headed by one of the final batch of P.L.M. 'C' class 4–4–0s, introduced in 1895. Most of this class of 4-cylinder compounds had this early form of streamlining (they were officially known as 'wind-cutters') and some survived to SNCF days. *["La Vie du Rail"*

The Railways of France

by J. B. Snell

The first public railway in France was an 8-mile line from St. Etienne to Andrézieux, on the River Loire, opened in 1828; it was acquired by the St. Etienne-Lyon company, who completed their 38-mile route down the other side of the watershed to the Rhône at Givors and Lyons between 1830 and 1832. The main traffic was coal; both the Andrézieux and Givors lines were originally worked by gravity power, with horses used to haul the empties back uphill, but in 1832 steam locomotives designed by Marc Séguin were placed in service. Both lines still flourish, though diverted in places; the constant falling gradient of the now-electrified Givors line is quite noticeable and allows the marshalling yard at Terrenoire to be very cheaply worked, since shunting engines are not needed.

But although France had railways very early, the system was slower to develop at first than in Britain for a variety of reasons; and the course of French railway history, together with the present status of the railway system, is so fundamentally different from the British story that some account of the rather complicated economic and legal background is essential before the subject can be properly understood.

There were two essential differences already before the start of the railway age. One was that France is a much larger country, with a more dispersed population; in 1800 it had 27 million inhabitants compared with Britain's 16 million (in 1958, by the way, the figures were 44 and 53 million respectively), and thus a density of population less than half ours. The other was that there was a considerable tradition of state action to improve inland transport. Whereas in Britain the private turnpike trusts had done most of the work in improving the national road system during the 18th century, in France the state took on this task and was just getting to grips with the job after the Napoleonic Wars. In 1815 the national trunk road network, the Routes Nationales, amounted only to 3,000 leagues (a league was $2\frac{1}{2}$ miles). In 1844 it comprised 8,628 leagues; and the secondary network of Routes Departmentales, or country roads, increased over the same period from some 2,000 to 9,146 leagues.

So although during the 1830s French opinion was well aware of the advantages of the railway, the economic problems of building a national system were daunting. The Liverpool and Manchester line might pay handsomely, but populous Lancashire was far more favourable ground than rural France. A first set of railway laws were passed in 1833, which among other things established the important principle that no company was to have absolute ownership of any railway; it could only hold a lease for not more than 99 years. Government rights of inspection and control, including setting maximum scales of charges, were also established. Certain short railways were built thereafter, including the first line in Paris (to St. Germain) in 1837, and the competing Left and Right Bank lines to Versailles, in 1839/40; there were several other railways in mining districts, but the most important was the first French main line, the 87-mile Strasbourg-Mulhouse-Basle, opened in 1841.

The fundamental change was brought about by the Law of June 11th, 1842, which established the geographical, the legal, and the financial basis of the national railway system. It proposed seven main lines radiating from Paris, plus two transversal routes; and under it the government undertook responsibility for the construction of the system. The state was to acquire the necessary land and build all earthworks, bridges, tunnels, and viaducts, together with stations and other buildings. It would then offer these to private companies on lease; the company would have to provide everything from the ballast up, track, rolling stock, locomotives, and signalling, and employ staff; leases conveying the right to operate would be given after competitive tender, and the company which offered the state the best terms and the shortest period of lease would win. It was estimated that this meant that of the total capital cost of the 2,500 kilometres of railway proposed, the state would contribute 400 million francs and private capital 320 million.

The seven lines to radiate from Paris were: to Belgium, via Amiens and Lille: to Strasbourg, via Nancy: to Marseilles, via Lyons: to Bordeaux and the Spanish frontier, via Orleans: to the Massif Centrale, also via Orleans: to Brittany, via Chartres and Rennes: and to Normandy via Rouen. The two transverse lines were to run from Bordeaux to Marseilles, via Toulouse and Narbonne: and from Dijon on the Paris-Marseilles line to the Strasbourg-Basle at Mulhouse.

From these proposals a number of companies developed, which by 1857 had amalgamated to form the six main-line undertakings which continued until 1938, and which in large part still survive as the various regions of the S.N.C.F. It was rapidly established that a company should have the monopoly of a given area, since the government in practice refused to authorise competitive lines. The six companies were as follows:

(i) *Chemin de fer du Nord.* This company received the concession for the Paris-Belgium route in 1842, and its history thereafter was exceedingly simple. It monopolized the area between the Paris-Hirson and Paris-le Tréport lines (inclusive), with one branch out of this zone from Amiens to Rouen.

(ii) *Chemin de fer de l'Est.* This company was incorporated in 1845 as the Chemin de fer de Strasbourg, when it obtained the concession for the Paris-Strasbourg trunk line. In 1854, when it also obtained the concession for the parallel main line from Paris to Basle via Chaumont, it changed its name, taking over the older railway from Basle to Strasbourg at the same time. It monopolized the area between the Nord and the Paris-Dijon line. Its corporate history was also simple, the main event being the loss of its railways in Alsace and Lorraine after the Franco-Prussian war in 1871. It is interesting to note that the victorious Prussians paid the company for these in cash. When France regained these properties in 1919, the railways (which had meanwhile been converted to right-hand working) were not returned to the Est but were worked by an independent government administration.

(iii) The *Paris-Lyon-Mediterranée.* The P.L.M. company was formed in

1857 by the amalgamation of several smaller concerns. It included principally the Paris-Lyon, established in 1845, and the Lyon-Mediterranée (1852), but this latter was already the result of an amalgamation which had included the Lyon-Avignon (1841), the Avignon-Marseille (1843) and the Grand'Combe-Beaucaire (1839). Its corporate history was also simple after 1857, the major events being a series of swallowings-up of smaller concerns so that it, too, came to monopolize its area.

(iv) The *Paris-Orléans*. The P-O was formed in 1838 simply to build the quite short line indicated by its title; but after 1842 it consolidated its position under the new regime and came to own the main lines from Paris via Tours and

The interior of the roundhouse at Nevers in 1863, showing the light and airy surroundings in which the 0–6–0 goods and 2–4–0 passenger engines were kept. *["La Vie du Rail"*

A mixed train at Questembert, on the South Brittany main line, around 1900, with inside- and outside-cylinder P.O. 2–4–0s Nos 133 and 747. *[J. B. Snell coll.*

Not all French Pacifics were compounds, by any means. The Midi had 20 of these handsome 2-cylinder simples built in 1921; they became SNCF class 231E (Mediterranean) and survived the war. *[F. Fleury coll.*

A Marseilles-Paris express leaving Dijon in 1929, with P.L.M. 231D class compound Pacific No. 231D.43. Some rebuilt members of this class are still running as class 231G (Nord). *[Dr. P. Ransome Wallis*

Poitiers to Bordeaux, and via Limoges to Toulouse, among others. The eastern boundary of its area, with the P.L.M., was definite enough after 1857 (see below), but its western boundary was less distinct and varied from time to time. It never owned all the railways between the Tours-Bordeaux line and the coast; on the other hand, it did own a main line to Nantes and Quimper, on the south side of the Breton peninsula and well off its home ground.

(v) *Chemin de fer de Midi.* This company was established in 1852 to work the transversal route from Bordeaux via Toulouse to the Mediterranean; but only as far as Sète, where there was to be an end-on junction with the P.L.M. It monopolized the area south of this line, but had very little track north of it; the main and anomalous exception was the much later and very mountainous branch from Béziers to Neussargues. There was an important test case in 1860 when the Midi asked for the right to build a competing route from Sète to Marseilles, which would give it access to this important city in its own right; by turning down this request the government firmly established the monopoly-zone principle. In 1934 the Midi and the P-O came to a joint working agreement like that between the South Eastern and the Chatham companies in Britain; they did not amalgamate, but thereafter the undertaking was run as one system and known as the P-O-Midi. At the same time the P-O relinquished the Quimper line beyond Nantes.

This accounts for five of the six companies. Before venturing into the complicated story of the sixth, one should give some account of the ill-fated Grand Central, which sank in 1857 but whose passing still leaves a trace on the S.N.C.F. timetable. This company obtained the concessions for lines from Bordeaux to Lyon via St Etienne, and from Paris to Nîmes via Clermont Ferrand. Access to Paris was to be by two routes, one over the P-O via Orleans and Vierzon to Saincaize, the other over a line joint with the P.L.M. from Saincaize to Moret-les-Sablons, 43 miles from Paris, and thence by running powers over the P.L.M. main line. The G.C. opened the line from Saincaize to Clermont Ferrand, but considering the disparity between its ambitious plans and the extremely hilly and rural country served it is hardly surprising it went bankrupt and failed. Its concessions were therefore divided in 1857 between the P-O and the P.L.M., the Moret-Saincaize-Clermont Ferrand-Nîmes route and everything east thereof going to the latter. But to this day certain expresses between Paris and Clermont Ferrand use the ex-P-O route via Vierzon.

The sixth main-line operator was the *Compagnie de l'Ouest,* which had its ups and downs. It was formed in 1855 by the amalgamation of the Normandy and Brittany companies, which held concessions for the Paris-Mantes-le Havre and Mantes-Cherbourg, and Paris-le Mans-Brest main lines respectively. The Ouest had a monopoly of this wholly rural area, north of the P-O's Tours-Nantes-Quimper line, but it was the poorest company of all and barely managed to keep afloat. However, its troubles were nothing to those of a number of small companies serving the area between Nantes and Bordeaux, west of the P-O, whose affairs were in a state of scandal; their concessions were withdrawn and they were taken over by the state. In 1883, since this Etat system remained unprofitable, the government decided to break its own rule in order to give them a transfusion of some main-line traffic. Certain branches were therefore exchanged with the P-O in order to establish a through route from Chartres to Bordeaux via Saumur; and with running powers over the Ouest from Chartres to Paris, a competing Paris-Bordeaux main line came into being. This was the only genuine example of railway competition in France. In 1909, when the Ouest company sank into insolvency yet again, the Etat administration took its lines over as well, and the two systems became one.

So much for the outline of company history. Something must now be said about the legal and economic framework within which the companies worked.

Although the Law of 1842 formed the basis of the main-line network, it did not work perfectly and left much ground uncovered. There was also very considerable variation in the terms by which the various working contracts were actually let. The government got the best deal out of the Nord, which agreed to repay the whole cost of construction on the main lines of the 1842 plan, and certain later lines as well, in return for a 99-year lease; so in effect the main lines in this prosperous and industrialized part of France were privately financed. The P-O also agreed to complete the works at its own expense on parts of the Bordeaux and Tours-Nantes main lines. On the other hand, in some cases the government got very much worse terms than had been envisaged in the legislation. Several of the lines in the west, notably from Paris to Chartres and beyond, had to be completed, opened, and run by the government for some time before a private company could be induced to put in a bid at all, while before the P.L.M. was formed parts of the Marseilles main line were in grave difficulties; the Avignon-Marseilles company had to be saved from ruin by a state guarantee of 7%! After 1851 the law was modified; the government extended all concessions to 99 years and began to ensure that the companies put their houses in order.

By the mid-1850s the 1842 plan was mainly achieved, and it was clear that more railways were going to be needed in other parts of the country. But since they were not principal inter-city connections, these new lines would not be so promising economically, and some kind of extra bait would be needed to tempt companies into contracting to work them. In 1859 it was therefore enacted that future construction would normally form a "nouveau réseau" on different terms; the state would build the earthworks, etc., as before (except that it would no longer erect stations and buildings) but it would also guarantee a dividend of 4·65% to the operating companies, provided that any sums paid out under this guarantee were repayable by a company out of any profits in excess of 5¾% earned over its whole undertaking.

This plan succeeded in getting these railways worked, and in fact cost the state little because with increasing prosperity the main lines of the "ancien réseau" were becoming profitable enough to support the costs of the guarantee on the "nouveau réseau". When, with increasing traffic, main-line improvements, bigger yards, more loops, and four-trackings began to be necessary, these were after 1868 regarded as part of the "nouveau réseau" and guaranteed accordingly. In 1883 the Nouveau and Ancien Reseaux were amalgamated, and the accounts combined; because they had never needed to claim under the guarantee, the wealthy Nord and P.L.M. companies were special cases, but generally the effect was that thenceforward the state guaranteed railway dividends at 5¾%, taking in return two-thirds of any greater profits. This system kept the finances of the main lines healthy until after 1918.

All the plans described so far were instituted to encourage the building of important main lines, whether the major trunk routes of the 1842 scheme (as enlarged by various later additions) or the only somewhat less important routes of 1859. There was still a need for branches and connections of a more local importance, and in 1865 a new legal framework was established for these. A distinction was drawn between lines of National Interest and lines of Local Interest; the former would still be financed under the earlier plans, but the latter would be treated in a new way. *Chemins de fer d'Intéret Local* were defined as those which were considered by the state to be of only local importance; they would rarely be longer than 30-40 km and would be lightly and cheaply built, with normally no through traffic. The central government would contribute up to half the cost of construction, including track, etc., according to the wealth of the area, and the local Departmental authorities could contribute the whole of the balance if they wished. The companies who worked these lines would have a 5% dividend guaranteed equally by the central and the local governments.

This legislation prompted considerable building of secondary railways, but led to various difficulties; it made for a hornet's nest of local political intrigue and scandal, and began to encourage the construction of competitive branches, which led to intolerable waste of money and was in absurd contradiction to the policy of refusing competitive main lines. So in 1879 the situation was set in order by the famous Freycinet Plan, which was a wide-ranging legal scheme also including provisions for the development of inland waterways. It proposed the construction of a further 6,009 miles of railways of National Interest (897 of which had already been authorised) which would complete the national system; part of this mileage was due to a declaration that it was in the National Interest that there should be a standard-gauge railway to every Sous-Préfecture, which meant in practice to every town of any size at all. Over and above this, there were to be a further 5,188 miles of Local Interest lines, serving remoter places. It was admitted that most of the total of 11,197 miles to be built would be uneconomic; however, it was considered that improved communication to all parts of the country was worth having for social reasons, and it was hoped that the economics would eventually improve. It was originally intended that all these lines should be built, equipped, and operated by the state; but in 1883 it was decided to allow them to be farmed out to companies in the usual way. A 3% dividend would be guaranteed; the company would have the right to retain $\frac{1}{3}$ of the working surplus, if any, and any deficit would be made up by the state. In fact, the National Interest lines went mainly to the six main-line companies, unless they were narrow-gauge, while the Local Interest lines stayed independent. Many *Départements* worked them themselves, but most were operated by small companies, some of which came to control numbers of local lines scattered about various parts of the country. Some of these concerns are still in business, although the railway side of their activities is not often very important nowadays.

Construction of railways under the Freycinet Plan went doggedly forward, until by 1914 it had been nearly finished; only two Sous-Préfectures, both in the Savoy Alps, had not been reached by rail at all, although several had metre-gauge lines only. The narrow-gauge boom after the 1870s, in fact, brought about a very great expansion of local railways over that envisaged by the Plan; not only were quite a number of National Interest lines built to metre gauge, but so were the great majority of the Local Interest ones, especially in the poorer areas; there were even a few two-footers. And instead of the 5,000-odd miles of local railway envisaged by Freycinet, 13,000 miles had actually been built by 1914, with another 4,000 under construction or proposed. About a third of the national total of railway route-mileage in 1914 was narrow-gauge.

The first world war marked a turning point, both in the shock it caused to the country and in the development of road transport. Although several new main lines were built in and into Alsace and Lorraine, construction of standard-gauge Freycinet Plan lines was not resumed, and the earthworks of several half-finished in 1914 still stand. Possibly the most spectacular of these is the line from le Puy to Lalevade d'Ardèche, through whose never-used 2-mile summit tunnel at St. Cirgues one may now drive, and which was to have included some extraordinary gyrations inside the crater of a primeval volcano involving two distinct spirals within a third; a mountain railway to outdo the Darjeeling-Himalayan! A few more metre-gauge lines were built, but the last was opened in 1925. Closures started five years later; for by 1930 the financial situation had been transformed for the worse by road competition and the slump.

So far as the main lines were concerned, the situation was bad enough. The Nord had lost its privileged position of never having asked for government money by way of guarantee, so in 1921 the accounts of all five surviving companies with the government were amalgamated and thereafter they were all treated the same. But with the effects of inflation and growing road competition things got worse, especially after 1929, and by 1935 only the Nord and the P.L.M. were making enough money even to cover the bare costs of operating (including, of course, in each case their comparatively few Freycinet lines). Overall, the state was having to pay out immense sums to cover losses and make up the guaranteed

The last ex-P.O. steam locomotives in service are the 2–8–2Ts of class 141TA. No. 467 climbing a 1 in 28 grade on the le Mont Dore branch with a train for Paris in 1967. [*Brian Stephenson*

Left: The last ex-Nord locomotives in service are the 141TC class 2–8–2Ts. No. 18 on a suburban push-and-pull train at Paris (Nord). [*Dr. P. Ransome-Wallis* *Right*: Typical of the once vast number of metre-gauge rural light railways was the Tramway de la Correze; 0–6–0T No. 8 follows every twist of the road near Lapleau with a maximum-load freight shortly before closure in 1959. [*J. B. Snell*

One of the more substantial, and still surviving, metre-gauge lines was that centred on Tulle, built jointly by the P-O and the Department of Corrèze 0–4–4–0T No. 104 on a Tulle-Argentat mixed at Laguenne. [*J. B. Snell*

The P.L.M.'s second 3,800-h.p. diesel, the twin-unit No. 262.BD.1 of 1937, on a Paris-Marseilles express before electrification. [*G. F. Fenino*

dividends. Many of the Freycinet lines had become unnecessary, particularly in the south and west, and a programme of closures was inescapable; while beginning to loom on the horizon was the fact that the companies' concessions were due to expire at various dates in the 1950s. So nationalization was decided on.

On January 1st, 1938, the railways belonging to the five main-line companies, plus the Etat and Alsace-Lorraine administrations, were taken over by the Société Nationale des Chemins de fer Français (S.N.C.F.). The state held 51% of S.N.C.F. shares; the five companies held the rest. No dividends would be paid on those shares held by the companies until 1955, but the companies would remain in legal existence until that date and would still be paid the guaranteed dividend; thereafter the companies were to be wound up and the S.N.C.F. shares distributed to their shareholders. Of course, the effect of inflation since 1938 meant that the shareholders then got about 2% of the value of their holdings. Still, they might be thought lucky to get that much; London & North Eastern shareholders, for instance, would have been unlikely to do any better if similar terms had been imposed in Britain.

The network of Local Interest lines was not nationalized; it would have been complicated to do this as there were so many different administrations (at one time well over a hundred), and rather pointless as many were already state-owned through the Departments. Instead, they were left to die; nothing was done about them. Many had already closed during the early 1930s, and there was a drastic purge in 1938/9 as part of the rationalization policy decided on jointly by local and central governments and the S.N.C.F., in which some 7,000 miles of railway were closed to passengers more or less overnight. However, during the second war and the Occupation, road transport was crippled and a number of lines closed but not yet dismantled reopened; thus about 7,000 miles of narrow-gauge railway, some half the original total, survived in 1947. But since then their decline has been merciless. Not one narrow-gauge Local Interest line now remains, and only six or seven National Interest ones. There are still a few standard-gauge Local Interest lines independently worked, but most of them handle freight only. On the other hand, so far as the S.N.C.F. is concerned, after the butchery of 1938-9 closures have been carried out slowly and with reluctance; suppression of a passenger service has occurred only infrequently, and total abandonments are rare. It is considered good policy to retain rural freight branches, on a minimum-maintenance basis, wherever reasonably possible, in order to provide a good national coverage for wagonload traffic. Of course, this allows many branches to be cut back or severed as through routes, since it is access to points that counts. On the other hand again, rationalization of main-line flows has been considerable, as outlined later.

This necessarily condensed account of French railway history omits much, but does at least demonstrate the danger of making easy comparisons between France and Britain. Above all, the present-day deficits are not by any means the same thing, although at present of the same order of magnitude in each country. The French railways have always been an overall financial liability to the state, even in their most prosperous years; but it was a charge accepted gladly because the country wanted the benefits that railways brought. Although there is some murmur about it now, the government still prefer to pay up rather than give the S.N.C.F. commercial freedom to reduce the deficit, since this would involve it in having to do things the government would dislike, from further closures on the one hand to charging mutilated veterans and the mothers of numerous families full price for their tickets on the other. Contrast this with the British position, where the railways were always expected to be fully self-supporting and the current deficit is regarded as a monstrous impropriety, an offence against nature, a dragon to be slain at all costs; let St. George's sword hack where it will, be St. George never so myopic.

In conclusion, it is interesting to consider a number of other aspects of

Left: One of the 1917-built American 2–8–0s, in this case by Baldwin: Ouest No. 1402 (later 140G.1402) on a Paris-le Croisic express at La Baule. [*O. J. Morris* *Right:* The last class of really elderly SNCF locomotives at work are the 130B 2–6–0s. These were originally built by the Est between 1859 and 1884, and rebuilt with larger boilers between 1906 and 1917; a number still work on the leased secondary lines around Gray. 130B.348 on a Chatillon-Chaumont freight near Veuxhalles in April, 1967. [*J. C. Beckett*

Compound Pacific No. 231K.30 leaving Boulogne Maritime with an express for Paris in 1964. These engines were rebuilt from P.L.M. class 231C, introduced in 1912. [*Brian Stephenson*

Left: P.L.M. 2–8–2 compound No. 141E.575 with the Ussel-Paris express near Eygurande-Merlines in 1966. [*J. C. Beckett* *Right:* A Paris-Quimper express near Malansac, headed by a 141P 2–6–2. [*J. C. Beckett*

railway operation where there are important differences between British and French practice.

The first is the question of electrification, combined with route rationalization. The French were in fact rather slow to start electrification, with the exception of the Midi company, which was a strong runner from the start and which commenced a policy of total electrification before the 1920s. This it carried to completion, including the conversion of some light-traffic branches in the Pyrenees, but for the remarkable omission of the Bordeaux-Montauban section of its main line, branches connecting with it, and the Narbonne-Port Bou route, all of which remain predominantly steam-worked to this day. The associated P-O also electrified its main lines, from Paris to Bordeaux between 1926 and 1939, and to Toulouse between 1935 and 1943; the Etat converted most of its Paris suburban lines quite early, and the Brittany main line as far as le Mans in 1937, while the P.L.M., after some early branch-line experiments, electrified the Culoz-Modane section of the main line to Italy via the Mont Cenis tunnel, which had long 1 in 33 grades, between 1929 and 1935. But that was all. The Nord and the Est had nothing. The whole of the rest of the present S.N.C.F. electrification, starting with the P.L.M. main line from 1950 and now covering most of the country, has been carried out in the last eighteen years. The technical aspects of this enormous work will be dealt with elsewhere; what should be noticed here is how the S.N.C.F. have been concerned, once a line was electrified, to concentrate as much traffic under the wires as possible. For instance, with the le Mans electrification, trains from Paris to Nantes and Quimper were diverted from their original P-O route via Tours to the Etat line via Chartres, and the le Mans-Angers branch upgraded to main-line status as a result. Similarly, the old Etat main line to Bordeaux via Saumur was progressively downgraded after the P-O line was electrified, singled throughout, and now consists of a series of end-to-end branches. The Nord once had an alternative route from Longueau (Amiens) to Paris, via Montdidier and Ormoy, mainly given over to 2–10–0s slogging along with heavy coal trains, leaving the main line via Creil clear for 4–6–2s on expresses; all through traffic now goes via Creil and the Montdidier route sees little service. There are other examples. However, there is one exception; the P.L.M. main line to Marseilles is paralleled throughout by an alternative route, also owned by the P.L.M., via Nevers, Moulins, the west bank of the Rhöne to Avignon, Cavaillon, and Port-de-Bouc. This was always used as an alternative route for freight, and because of the growth of traffic, even electrified the main line via Dijon cannot handle it all; so to this day a substantial amount of freight is still steam-worked on the alternative line, especially north of Lyon.

Another aspect of electrification policy is highly important, and little appreciated as yet in Britain. On a busy line, electric traction is in every way to be preferred to diesel traction; but the margin of preference is not great enough to justify the heavy capital outlay of electrification as opposed to continued use of diesels. Therefore, if one wishes to electrify one makes do with steam power in the interim. Any dieselization meanwhile will destroy the case for electrification, and the railway will be left permanently with the second-best. This great truth seems just about to dawn in Britain; far too late, of course.

A second difference is in the pattern of long-distance passenger services. The best trains have always been on the lines radiating from Paris, plus the Midi; other services were and still are distinctly inferior, although provincial centres like Lyons and Strasbourg do have some reasonable cross-country trains (e.g. Lyons-Bordeaux, Lyons-Nantes, Strasbourg-Nice). The original pattern of the 1850s was to have a day train and a night train, the former leaving very early so as to get there before midnight. Even though there have been vast accelerations since, allowing mid-day and even afternoon departures on long runs, the old pattern still forms the foundation of the timetable. However, since the war there has been a new element added; evening departures running at the highest possible speed, often with lightweight extra-fare trains, to give the latest possible start after business hours and an arrival around midnight. Originally these workings were by high-speed diesel railcars, but the business soon became too much for them, and after a brief and hectic period of steam working (the Paris-Strasbourg flyer, consisting of lightweight pneumatic-tyred stock, was hauled after 1948 by a jazzed-up 1906 4–6–0, streamlined and converted to oil-firing), the main ones are now electric locomotive-hauled, with some quite obscure but very fast connections still railcar-worked. In this way it is possible to leave Paris for cities as far off as Bordeaux (363 miles) at 18.45 (arr. 23.37), Brest (388 miles) at 19.00 (arr. 01.00), Lyons (320 miles) at 19.25 (arr. 23.33), Marseilles (536 miles) at 17.00 (arr. 00.32), Strasbourg (315 miles) at 19.05 (arr. 23.07), and Toulouse (443 miles) at 18.00 (arr. 24.00); compare leaving London for Glasgow (401 miles) at 16.05 (arr. 22.50). The Toulouse train is the "Capitole", allowed to run at especially high speeds and since 1967 at as much as 125 m.p.h. on the 44-mile Les Aubrais (Orléans)-Vierzon section; this by way of proving new equipment for wider use elsewhere. On the other hand, the general policy of running fast, but very heavy and rather infrequent trains, is beginning to look a little shopworn nowadays. Admirable from the point of view of railway economy to have 18 well filled coaches howling along at 87 m.p.h.; less attractive for the customer, with the alternatives of car and plane increasingly available, if this is the only train for four hours either way. There are some signs, particularly in the North, that the S.N.C.F. is beginning to appreciate this.

Seasonal variations in traffic, about which we heard so much from Dr. Beeching in Britain, are not unknown in France either. The S.N.C.F. experience far sharper and shorter summer and Christmas holiday peaks than B.R. ever did, but they handle them with a smaller fleet of spare coaches and so far from working to rid themselves of this traffic they take pride in their ability to meet the demands made on them. Penny-foolish perhaps; but arguably pound-wise.

A third difference is in the pattern of signalling and the related discipline of train running. Classical nineteenth-century French signalling was organized on principles different to British ones; different types of signal were used to convey the different messages "you are catching up with the train in front" and "stop, because there is some conflicting movement ahead of you" (a distinction not made in Britain), while the indication to the driver exactly which track he was going to be switched onto was not attempted. After all, he didn't have to steer; why should he worry, so long as his maximum speed was indicated to him? Older signalling, known as mechanical signalling, used and uses a semaphore to give the first sort of message, and a red-and-white chequerboard to give the second. A semaphore at danger generally means "stop and proceed with caution"; a "*carré*" when visible could never be passed at all (when "clear" it was turned edge-on so as to disappear). Speed restrictions and distant warnings were indicated by other types of signal, the former often moveable and interlocked with the points. The same principles have been followed with the automatic colour-light signals now almost universal on main lines. With these (as by night with mechanical signalling) a single red light means "stop and proceed with caution" except where there is a junction or a tunnel ahead, and a double red light means "stop absolutely"; while all main lines, whether the signalling has been modernized or not, are equipped with automatic train control.

So far so good; but the most important part of all this is the rigorous enforcement of speed limits, combined with staff incentives, based on the Flaman Recorder, which has enabled train running even with steam power to reach a degree of precision that still escapes B.R. The general maximum speed limit is 140 km./h. (87 m.p.h.) but certain lines and certain types of locomotive have lower or occasionally higher limits imposed. Enginemen, whether steam, diesel, or electric, receive a bonus for fuel economy which is worth earning; but they receive a larger bonus for recovery of lost time, which gives a strong incentive to make every effort

The southbound "Mistral" at Avignon, with D.C. Electric No. BB.9275. [*A. Davenport*

One of the varieties of railcar introduced during the 1950s for high-speed services on cross-country routes was this twin-engined 850-hp type, shown here with trailer on a Grenoble-Bordeaux working near Ussel. [*J. C. Beckett*

when running late (with us, of course, they have the prospect of earning overtime). Furthermore, they receive a very thorough training in the mechanical and scientific principles on which their locomotives work, so that they really can get the best out of them. On the other hand, the speed attained at every point on the run, together with a record of every signal met at "caution" or "danger", is printed onto a paper roll in the Flaman Recorder, which is examined in detail; any transgression of speed limits leads to trouble at once, while failure to acknowledge a "caution" aspect is a serious matter and overshooting a "danger" signal is a crime for which there is no forgiveness whatever, and rightly; that driver never enters a locomotive cab again.

This account of the S.N.C.F. has perhaps done little to describe the physical atmosphere of the French railway system today, but there is a simple remedy for this; go and see for yourself. It is no longer quite the *stupor mundi* it was, say in the mid-1950s; in some ways, others have caught up and even overtaken. The fact remains that in the first 21 years of its existence, from 1938 to 1959, S.N.C.F. passenger-miles increased by 44.8% and freight ton-miles by 102%; while its operations were carried out by 9,350 locomotives instead of 19,400, with half the number of passenger coaches, with 357,000 wagons instead of 508,000, and with 357,000 employees instead of 514,000. Such a stupendous increase in productivity remains unparalleled anywhere, and the French railwaymen still has a job to be proud of. The fleet of passenger coaches is getting a bit elderly, but they are vastly solid, well-maintained, and smooth-running, and long, heavy, well-filled trains still work into stations often quite modern, and almost always generously laid out and uncongested. Freight trains are enormous to British eyes, and roar along (even behind steam engines) with only a two-man crew; guards are only employed on pick-up workings where intermediate shunting has to be done. Dining cars, and those sandwichmen who come along the corridors, may be expensive, but the restaurants on the stations are often among the best eating-places in town. In short, the S.N.C.F. still believes in itself, and its customers (therefore; inevitably; naturally;) are of the same opinion.

French Motive Power

by Dr. P. Ransome-Wallis

According to statistics published by the S.N.C.F., the percentage of traffic (in ton-miles) moved by steam locomotives has fallen from 75.1% in 1950 to 10% at the end of 1967. During the same period, the proportion handled by electric traction increased from 22.9% to 73.5%, and by diesel traction (including railcars) from 2% to 16.5%; however, most of the increase in the diesel proportion has taken place in the last 3 or 4 years of the period.

It has been the policy of the S.N.C.F. to replace steam by electric traction wherever the traffic justified, or would in future justify, the initial cost of the fixed installations. However, the comparative cheapness of 25 kV A.C. electrification, together with the successful introduction of bi-current locomotives, have greatly modified the original criteria for deciding which lines were to be electrified, and increased the number converted very considerably. On lines where electrification could not be justified, diesel traction was to replace steam; but this policy has till now had a lower priority, allowing various technical improvements to diesel locomotives to be developed at a deliberate pace.

Steam Locomotives now in Service

All steam locomotives in France are scheduled to be withdrawn by 1971. Thus will end the story of the finest locomotive work the world has ever seen; a story of highly efficient, but often highly complicated, machines, worked by some of the best trained and most competent locomotive men there have ever been. A lot of superlatives, perhaps, but nobody who has studied steam locomotive work in many countries will deny their truth.

The run-down of steam in France has been carefully planned to avoid, so far as possible, any scrapping of locomotives before the expiry of their economic lives. There have been some exceptions, but at no time has there been the wholesale slaughter of near-new machines and the panic buying of new and untried diesel or electric power for political reasons that has been witnessed in one, at least, of France's neighbour countries.

In France more than anywhere, the principle of "one man, one engine" or "machine titulaire" was adhered to and a driver might have the same engine for 12 or 15 years, staying with it if he so wished, while it went through shops at the time of "Grande Réparation" every 175,000 miles; for these men were engineers as well as drivers. But with the present situation it has no longer been possible to maintain this principle, and the common user system ("la banalité") has become almost universal. Although the standard of performance remains high, there is now some falling off in cleanliness and attention to detail. Needless to say, it is in the compound locomotives that one notices most these little deficiencies, for if ever locomotives deserved the description "individual", it was the French compounds. Those which still survive, giving excellent accounts of themselves, are the more straightforward and uncomplicated machines emanating from basic P.L.M. designs. The locomotives of Chapelon, the C.M.E. of the P-O, have now all disappeared; but it is possible that there may have been some question of personalities and company traditions here. There was for many years in the S.N.C.F. a clash like that we had between the Derby and Crewe factions in the 1920s, or Gresley and Thompson at a later date. Chapelon was trained in a different school from the renowned Louis Armand as well as from the powerful hierarchy of the PLM locomotive engineers, and this may explain why as one of the world's greatest locomotive engineers he never became supreme head of the

2–10–0 No. 150P.8; these engines, developed from a Nord design, were introduced by the SNCF in 1939.
[*Brian Stephenson*

The final variant of class 141R differs externally in having a complete set of Boxpok driving wheels and Delta truck for the rear bogie. 141R.1272, built in Montreal, at the head of a Calais-Paris express. [*Brian Stephenson*

A Boulogne-Paris boat train near St Josse, headed by 141R.150, built by the Lima Locomotive Co. [*J. C. Beckett*

Perhaps the most impressive-looking French passenger locomotives were the Est compound 4–8–2s of class 241A, introduced in 1925; although as hand-fired machines they were not quite the equal of the later 241P. 241A.25 on a local train, passing an Est 4–6–0 of class 230B. [*Dr. P. Ransome-Wallis*

The Paris (Austerlitz)-Clermont Ferrand-le Mont Dore "Thermal Express" at Vierzon; 241P.10 has just taken over from an electric locomotive. [*Brian Stephenson*

S.N.C.F. Locomotive Department but ended his career as "Chef des Etudes des Locomotives à Vapeur".

Among the last surviving compounds are some of the ex-P.L.M. Pacifics, mainly around Calais. The P.L.M. was, in 1909, the second European railway to introduce Pacifics; the P-O beat it by a few weeks. After comparative trials between 4-cylinder simples and compounds, the latter were preferred, and the P.L.M. built 85, with superheating and all cylinders in line, between 1912 and 1921. These were P.L.M. class 231.C. In 1924 they were much improved by being fitted with trefoil blast pipes and A.C.F.I. feedwater pumps and heaters, and in 1930 improved further still with new cylinders, wider and more direct steam passages, and double blastpipes and chimneys. 83 engines were so dealt with, and became class 231.K; some of these still survive.

The P.L.M. built 285 more compound Pacifics, classes 231D and 231F between 1922 and 1935; the main difference from the earlier engines was that they did not have independent cut-off for HP and LP cylinders, but it was instead arranged in a fixed ratio between the two sets of valve gear. These engines were, again, rebuilt similarly during the 1930s, becoming series 231.G. Some of these are also still in service.

During the last few years a number of other companies, designs of Pacific have become extinct. Most notable were the ex-P-O machines of class 321E, some of which had been rebuilt from earlier engines by Chapelon in 1934 while others were built new, for both P-O and Nord companies, to the revised design shortly afterwards. More numerous were the ex-Etat types, classes 231D and 231G notably, which had a similar history of rebuilding. But every pre-1938 railway had a set of 4–6–2 compounds of its own design, most of which were rebuilt on Chapelon principles during the 1930s and 1940s. It should be noted here that the S.N.C.F. never had a national code of steam locomotive classifications, which remained largely as they were in company days, except to standardize the method of classification; thus different regions might possess quite different locomotives both classified "231.E" or "231.G". The only uniformity was to reserve P and later letters for classes built for or designed by the S.N.C.F.

Only two series of compounds (both 4-cylinder designs) were built by the S.N.C.F.; both are still active. 318 mixed-traffic 2—8—2s of class 141P were built between 1942 and 1952; these engines have given a good account of themselves but have been displaced in the diminishing field of main-line work by the rather larger 141Rs (see below) and relatively few survive, chiefly at Chaumont. The other series are the most powerful steam locomotives still at work in France, indeed in Europe; the 241P express passenger 4–8–2s, 35 of which were built between 1947 and 1949. These fine machines have mechanical stokers, a boiler pressure of 20 atmospheres (291 lbs. per sq. in.) and a tractive effort of 45,100 lbs. They are basically of P.L.M. design; that company, coincidentally with the Est, having introduced a series of express passenger 4–8–2s in 1925. These original machines were hand-fired and had driving wheels of only 5' 10" diameter, but in 1930 the P.L.M. built one compound 4–8–2 with 6' 6½" wheels, a different cylinder layout, and mechanical stoker; and this solitary machine formed the prototype for the 241Ps, although they have strengthened frames and other modifications. It is probable that if Chapelon had had his way they would have been 3-cylinder compounds and, possibly, 4–8–4s like his one great experimental machine of 1948, 242.A.1. The remaining 241Ps work on the Clermont Ferrand and Paris-Basle main lines, with perhaps a few survivors at Le Mans and Nantes in the Western Region.

The most numerous class of steam locomotives, now accounting for over half the total stock, are the American and Canadian-built mixed-traffic 2–8–2s of class 141R; 1,340 of these were built between 1945 and 1947, although 17 never got to France as they were lost at sea with the SS *Belpamela*. With driving

241P.28 at the head of a Paris-Basle express, leaving Chaumont in April, 1967. [*B. A. Seaton*

The Lille-Dijon express leaving Chaumont behind an SNCF 68000-class 2,700-hp diesel-electric, complete with steam-heat van, in April, 1967. [*J. C. Becket*

The ex-LB&SCR J2 class 4–6–2T, No. 2326, as running in SR colours in 1947. [J. M. Jarvis

wheels only 5' 5" in diameter they are limited to 65 mph, but they are to be found in all parts of the country on all types of work. They are typical of American locomotive practice of the period: two cylinder-simples with cast steel frames or "engine beds", power reverse, chime whistles. 719 had mechanical stokers for coal firing and 604 were oilburners, though some were later changed to coal. There were a number of differences between various batches from various builders; for example, in the variation between plain spoked and Boxpok driving wheels, the design of the rear pony truck, and whether fitted with plain or single Kylala blast pipes. The 141Rs were the first main-line locomotives to be operated on a common-user basis; few, if any, were ever assigned to one crew.

Other surviving mixed-traffic engines include some ex-P.L.M. compound 2–8–2s, class 141.E, and some ex-Etat simple 2–8–2s, class 141.C. The 4–6–0s are now extinct; the last were the ex-P-O 230.G class simples, although the 230.D compounds on the Nord were, for a 1910 design, surprisingly numerous until 2 or 3 years ago.

The most numerous surviving freight locomotives are 2–8–0s and 0–8–0s. Most of the former are series 140.C, simple engines built by a number of firms (including the North British Locomotive Co.) to the order of the French government between 1913 and 1917; there were at one time 370 of these. From 1917 to 1921 certain American builders supplied more than 1,500 heavy 2–8–0s to France, but the last of these was scrapped some years ago. The surviving 0–8–0s are all of class 040.D, and are members of a very large family, originating on the Prussian State Railways in 1910 as class G8.1; between then and 1919 no fewer than 5,260 were built, making them one of the most numerous locomotive types on record. After 1918 they were sent as reparations to many countries and there are few parts of Europe and the Middle East where they have not worked. The 2–10–2s of the P.L.M. and the Alsace-Lorraine have long gone; the last 2–10–0s were compounds of Nord design, but with mechanical stoker and other improvements, class 150.P, and were withdrawn in 1967, putting an end to a wheel arrangement found on every line except the Midi and the Ouest.

Among the remaining tank locomotives, the P-O 2–8–2Ts of class 141.TA are notable. These originated with a series built by the Swiss Locomotive Co. in 1911 for service on the steep grades in the Massif Centrale; between then and 1923 190 were constructed, some again by North British. 39 went to Morocco during the 1930s, but others still work in their original territory. Another quite different series of 2–8–2T are those built for the Nord between 1932 and 1935, class 141.TC. These were designed to work push-and-pull trains of up to 500 tons (or 10 coaches) in Paris suburban service, a task they still perform; electro-pneumatic control gear allows them to be driven from the other end of the train. The Etat's 2–8–2Ts for similar duty in the western suburbs, the 3-cylinder 141.TDs, have recently been replaced by electrification, but some of the Est's equivalents, again 2–8–2Ts but again quite different, class 141.TB, still work out of Paris (Bastille) pending electrification. And a few of the 151.TQ 2–10–2Ts built in 1939 for freight service on the Paris Ceinture line still survive at Boulogne.

The P.L.M.'s Paris suburban trains, as well as locals in other parts of the system, were worked by 4–8–4Ts of class 242.TA; 4-cylinder compounds introduced in 1927. Some still run in the Lille and Strasbourg areas, although no longer on push-and-pull work. Finally, mention must be made of the very fine 0–10–0Ts of series 050.TQ, built in 1948-9. This design dates back to a number of engines built for the P-O and the Midi in 1908, with only small modifications. They are unusual for 0–10–0s in that the drive is to the fourth coupled axle, necessitating the use of very long piston rods.

Diesel Locomotive Development

Diesel motive power on the S.N.C.F. can be classified under four heads: (1) Autorails; all types of railcars and railbuses. There is such a variety of these

A Bordeaux-Nantes express headed by a CC.65000 diesel (then classified as 060.DB) in 1959. [*J. B. Snell*

Lightweight diesel No. BB.63141 on a branch freight near Lens. *Dr. P. Ransome-Wallis*

Le Havre-Paris express at Sotteville, with diesel No. BB.67054. [*Brian Stephenson*

that it is impossible to describe them here. The commonest types are single cars with one sufficiently powerful engine, generally in the carbody, to allow them to haul several trailers; but there are a great number of designs, many dating back to the 1930s, and ranging up to the modern high-speed Trans-Europe-Express or R.G.P. lightweight sets. (2) Locotracteurs: small 4- or 6-wheeled shunting locomotives. Again, these are too numerous to describe. (3) Mixed traffic and larger shunting locomotives, analagous to the American "road-switcher". (4) Main line and express locomotives.

The power output of all diesel locomotives is generally quoted in kilowatts produced by the generator, according to the U.I.C. rating; this is equivalent to 70-80% of the nominal diesel engine power output for locomotives, 75-85% for locotracteurs and 80% for railcars (for conversion for British comparisons, 1 horsepower is .746 kilowatts, but it should be remembered that we quote the diesel engine output in gross, so that a 2,000-hp. British diesel would be rated around 1,500 h.p. (or 1,100 kW) in France).

The first internal-combustion locomotives were a series of locotracteurs built for the P.L.M. in 1917, and many hundreds of these small machines have been built since; each of the six companies had some. But only eight more powerful diesels were built in France before 1939, all for the P.L.M. Six were shunters of around 600 h.p., the earliest of which appeared in 1932; the seventh was a remarkable machine. It was an express passenger locomotive, built in 1936 for service between Paris and Nice; it comprised two identical 1-F (in steam parlance, 2–12–0) units permanently coupled back to back. Each unit contained two 6-cylinder Sulzer diesels driving a single generator, powering three traction motors having two armatures each, so that there was in effect independent power to each driving axle. The total output of the whole locomotive was 3,800 h.p., and it was able to haul 600-ton trains at 81 m.p.h. A somewhat similar machine was placed in service in 1937. Both were successful, and ran on the P.L.M. main line until they were withdrawn in 1954, following electrification.

During the post-war reconstruction period main-line dieselization was started by 100 American 660-hp six-axle machines, built by Baldwin-Westinghouse in 1946-7. All are still in service, mainly on freight trip working. They are now classified as the A1A-A1A.62000 series. After 1949 a series of 375-hp six-wheeled diesel-electric shunters, class C.61000, surprisingly similar in appearance to our own English Electric machines, made its appearance; there are also a number of similar but cabless locomotives capable of being worked in multiple, like the "cow-and-calf" American arrangement, for heavy shunting in humps, etc.

The first standard class of diesels, intended mainly for service on secondary and branch lines with limited axleloading restrictions, are now class BB.63000; a "road-switcher" type with a single cab. Starting in 1953, they have been supplied by several builders and with several differences in detail, and by 1968 the class numbered 1,059 locomotives. According to the make of engine employed, power rating varies from 725 to 825 h.p.; speed is limited to 50 m.p.h., but these useful 66-ton machines do a great deal of work.

The next class, now CC.64000, appeared in 1955; this comprises 35 machines for freight haulage on the difficult lines of the Grande Ceinture round Paris, where 2,000 ton trainloads are commonplace. These engines replaced no fewer than 80 2–10–2Ts. Rated at 1,500 h.p. they are powered by one Sulzer 12DA 12-cylinder engine, the cylinders being arranged in side-by-side banks of six driving two crankshafts, which are geared together. Each of the six axles is motored; these 120-ton heavy freight locomotives were the first "cab" units (i.e. with two cabs) in France, apart from the two P.L.M. giants of 1936-7.

Series CC 65.000, twenty of which were built between 1956-59, were mixed-traffic main-line locomotives which were used to replace main-line steam in the Ouest region between the Loire and the Gironde, centered at La Rochelle. Although there is an external family resemblance, they are quite different to the

Ceinture locomotives; their total U.I.C. rating, in horsepower, is around 1,400 and this is provided by two separate 12- or 16-cylinder diesel engines in each locomotive, made by M.G.O. or de Dietrich respectively. Although their performance is satisfactory in service, the cost and complication of this arrangement appears to have reinforced the determination of the S.N.C.F. to soft-pedal main-line dieselization until simpler and more powerful machines were developed.

The next class appeared in 1959; series BB.66000. These are an enlarged variety of class BB.63000, with similar appearance and layout; depending on the make of engine, they are rated up to 1,400 h.p., and can run at up to 75 m.p.h. They undertake many different duties, from shunting to working fast passenger trains; when in passenger service in winter, they must be attached to a "fourgon chaudière" or boiler-van for train-heating, but the most recent batch (BB.66.401-475) are being fitted with electric train-heating equipment and more powerful diesel engines and generators to allow for this extra demand. These locomotives have given excellent service in France and have been exported to several other countries, including Yugoslavia where they are now being built under license.

It was not until seven years after the appearance of the CC.65000 class that any more "cab"-type diesels were built, but two different varieties appeared in 1963, both intended to replace the fleet of compound Pacifics still working important expresses. Both have a very similar and rather stylized appearance, and mark the start of a new era of diesel locomotive development, in which many lessons learnt in electric practice have been applied. But apart from these resemblances, the two classes are very different internally.

The BB.67000 is a mixed-traffic locomotive, powered by a single 16-cylinder engine capable of developing 2,400 h.p. but limited in service to 2,000; giving a U.I.C. horsepower of around 1,500. It is carried on two four-wheeled monomotor bogies, with a single traction motor geared to both axles in each; furthermore the gearing provides two speed ratios, suitable for freight or for passenger service; either can be engaged from the cab through a pneumatic control while the locomotive is stationary. The maximum speed attainable in low gear is 56 m.p.h., but in passenger service 84 m.p.h. can be reached. They weigh only 80 tons, and to keep within this limit steam heating equipment had to be omitted from the first 124 locomotives. However, the 96 now on order have been modified to include a.c./d.c. transmission and provision for electric train heating.

Class A1A.A1A.68000, on the other hand, 110 strong, are express passenger locomotives. They are powered by 12-cylinder engines which develop 2,930 h.p. so giving a U.I.C. rating around 2,200 h.p. The weight of these locomotives in working order is 106 tonnes, but this includes a train-heating boiler. There is normally a load of 18 tonnes on each of the two driving axles of each bogie, and 17 tonnes on the intermediate axle, but when the locomotive is allocated to service on lines where heavier loadings are permissible it is possible to provide increased adhesion by altering the geometry of the bogie suspension in the depot. There is then a load of 20 tonnes on the driving, and 13 on the intermediate, axles. Furthermore, because of the weight transference experienced while starting and accelerating a heavy train, which has the effect in these machines of transferring up to 3 tonnes from the front to the rear bogie, provision has been made for making a further increase in the adhesion on the leading bogie by means of pneumatic equipment controlled from the cab for relieving the carrying axle of a further part of its load.

These two classes appear to have solved the problem of replacing steam locomotives of moderate power. But the replacement of the largest steam locomotives in diesel traction areas began only in 1964 and is far from being completed. Apart from using the 67.000 or 68.000 series in tandem, which the S.N.C.F. regards as uneconomic, there are at the time of writing only four diesels in service in France which can improve upon the sustained power output of a 141R in freight service, or of a 241P working an 800-ton train on a mile-a-minute schedule. And since the S.N.C.F. have declared their intention to work trains of the same or greater weight on faster schedules, it is obvious that much more powerful locomotives are essential.

These four locomotives are of two types. Series BB.69000 are diesel-hydraulics each powered by two engines identical to those used singly in the BB.67000 series. They weigh only 84 tons, and have a traction power output of 4,120 h.p., but no provision for train heating; they were placed in service in 1964. Series CC.70000 use the same diesel engines, again two per locomotive, but have a.c./d.c. electric transmission, with an unusual type of alternator in which one diesel engine drives the rotor and the other the "revolving stator" or armature in the opposite direction; and they are mounted on six-wheeled change-speed monomotor bogies. They weigh 118 tons, and have provision for electric train heating.

As a result of experience gained with these machines, hydraulic transmission has been discarded and a.c./d.c. transmission decided on; however, further construction was postponed until a single diesel engine of sufficient output to replace the two used in each of the experimental machines was available. An engine with a U.I.C. rating of 3,600 h.p. has now been developed and will be installed in the 38 locomotives of series CC.72000 due for delivery in 1968. Series BB.71000, introduced meanwhile, is a small and lightweight "road-switcher" type, intermediate between the six-wheeled C.61000 and the BB.63000; the thirty locomotives of this class are unusual in having coupling rods on their bogies.

Electrification and Electric Locomotives

The S.N.C.F. now operate five different systems of electrification on standard-gauge lines; three of these date back to company days. The oldest system, using 750v D.C. with third rail, is in use on certain ex-Ouest suburban lines out of Paris, originating with the Invalides-Versailles (Rive Gauche) line, electrified since its opening in 1900; between 1924 and 1936 most of the shorter suburban lines out of St. Lazare station were also converted. The third rail is of G-section, with collector shoes bearing up against the underside of the top lip; it is therefore immune from icing-up trouble. The P.L.M., after experimenting with an A.C. system, adopted 1,500v D.C. for the Culoz-Modane scheme in 1929, in this case using third rail on plain line and, for reasons of safety, overhead wire in stations. This arrangement still exists, so that locomotives running south of Culoz need collector shoes. The P.L.M. third rail is top contact, like ours, but icing-up and electrocutions are both prevented by means of a wooden casing around and above the third rail, allowing only a narrow slit on the inside for entry of collector gear. The Midi in 1912 installed an experimental 12kV $16\frac{2}{3}$ cycle A.C. overhead system on the Perpignan-Villefranche branch; this is still in operation, with its original motor coaches, for passenger trains, but the last of the locomotives was withdrawn in 1959.

However, the Midi came to prefer the 1,500 volt D.C. overhead system, the first section of which it installed in 1914 on the Toulouse-Bayonne line between Tarbes and Montrejeau, which included 6 miles of 1 in 30. After 1918, as we have seen, it adopted a policy of total electrification on this system, which it largely carried out. This decision in turn influenced the P-O's choice of the same system for its Paris-Orleans-Vierzon scheme in 1926, replacing its pre-1914 600v D.C. third-rail installation in the Paris suburbs; and with the P.L.M. and then the Etat following suit, the latter with the le Mans scheme in 1937, the 1,500 v D.C. overhead system was well established as standard; and so it remained until the 1950s.

However, the S.N.C.F. was impressed by the economies that could be made by using high-voltage A.C. at industrial frequency, and by way of experiment and proof electrified part of the Aix les Bains—La Roche sur Foron branch in Savoy on the 20kV (later increased to 25kV) 50 cycles A.C. overhead system. These trials showed that despite certain difficulties, notably interference with telecommunications, the first cost of installing this system was 20-25% lower than D.C., with unimportant additions to running cost; the savings were due to the lighter wires and structures needed and the greater distances possible between sub-stations. So not only was this pilot scheme extended, but the decision was taken to use 25kV A.C. to electrify the main lines in the Nord and Est regions, hitherto not considered for conversion as they served an area where coal was cheap and plentiful. Starting almost at once with the Valenciennes-Thionville line, a cracking pace was set, and for the next 10-12 years an average of between 3 and 4 route-miles per week were electrified.

Left: The last class of SNCF electric locomotives with separate driving and carrying wheels were the 5,550-hp 2D2.9100 class of 1950. No. 9119 enters Dijon with a Paris-Nice express. [*Brian Stephenson*

Right: The Dunkirk-Basle train entering Valenciennes, with 25kV AC electric No. BB.1201. [*S.N.C.F.*

Further extensions of D.C. electrification were also undertaken, notably the completion to Marseilles in 1962, but the recent development of locomotives able to work on both systems at full power and to change from one to the other at speed probably means that there will be no further new D.C. schemes. However, there is no thought of converting D.C. lines to A.C., as B.R. have done; once the D.C. equipment is in, there is nothing whatever to be gained by the expensive task of alteration, and running costs would be marginally increased with no improvement in performance. Thus the le Mans electrification has been extended with A.C. to Rennes, and the Marseilles similarly to Ventimiglia; changeover points exist also north and west of Dijon as well as the original one at Aix-les-Bains. Otherwise, a line drawn from le Mans through Paris, north of Dijon, to Dole and Geneva marks a boundary. Northwards, all electrification is A.C.; southwards, all is D.C.

There is unfortunately no space to give an adequate account of S.N.C.F. electric motive power, which includes many machines, ancient and modern, of great technical interest. One reason for this is that there are so many varieties. The pioneering work done both with D.C. in the early days and with A.C. more recently led to the construction of many experimental types, which have often remained in service. On the D.C. lines alone, 58 classes of locomotive worked in 1960, 19 of which consisted of one or two machines only, and the proliferation of A.C. types is still proceeding. There are also many varieties of electric railcar and multiple units. The two S.N.C.F. metre-gauge lines, both electrified with third rail D.C., should not be overlooked; the Chamonix line is especially memorable in that until 1958 every one of its 161 pieces of rolling stock, from coaches down to vans, wagons, flattrucks, and snowploughs, was a powered four-wheeler capable of being driven independently.

In general, for high-speed work each of the companies, and the S.N.C.F. until the 1950s, preferred locomotives with driving wheels mounted in a rigid or articulated frame. but all except the P.L.M. built double-bogie eight-wheelers as a rule for freight and mixed traffic work. With the development of powerful traction motors sufficiently small to be mounted in bogies, driving-wheel designs became obsolete after 1950 and so are unknown on A.C. lines. An example of progress in express locomotive design can be given by comparing the P.L.M. 2CC2s of 1929, remarkable engines for their day in developing 5,530 h.p. in a total weight of 159 tonnes, with the BB 9200 class of 1957, 5,570 h.p. and 80 tonnes. Further developments in recent years have been on the lines of (i) monomotor bogies, in which both axles, being driven by the same motor, have less tendency to slip, and in which change-speed gearing allows the same locomotive to perform advantageously in both freight and passenger service; (ii) providing transformers, etc., to allow through running over two or more systems of electrification, thus passing at speed not only from French D.C. to A.C., as we have seen, but to the German 15kV 16⅔ cycles A.C. or the Belgian 3,000v D.C.; the CC 41000 class are equally at home in all four cases.

Particulars of the most numerous electric locomotive classes, i.e. those with over 20 members, are given in tabular form below. As with steam engines, the wheel arrangement is prefixed to the number. All D.C. locomotives are numbered below 9999; 25kV A.C. machines are in the 10,000 series, and thereafter the first number indicates the number of systems the locomotive can work on, i.e.; 20,000 series—25kV 50 cycles A.C. and 15kV 16⅔ cycles A.C.; 25,000 series—25kV A.C. and 1,500 v D.C.; 30,000 series—25kV A.C., 1,500 vD.C., 3,000v D.C.; 40,000 series—all four systems.

Class	*Company*	*Date*	*No. in service*	*Horsepower (1-hr.)*
D.C. Lines				
2D2 5000	Midi	1932	24	3,900
2D2 5400	Etat	1937	22	4,230
2D2 5503, 5538, 5546	P-O	1933	48	4,230
2D2 9100	S.N.C.F.	1950	35	5,550
BB 1, 101	P-O	1924	160	1,900
BB 300	P-O	1938	55	2,040
BB 900	Etat	1936	34	2,420
BB 4100, 4200, 4600, 4700	Midi	1928	205	1,780*
BB 8100	S.N.C.F.	1949	171	3,190
BB 8500	S.N.C.F.	1964	36	3,500†
BB 9200	S.N.C.F.	1957	92	5,570
BB 9400	S.N.C.F.	1958	135	3,130
CC 7100	S.N.C.F.	1952	58	5,060
A.C. Lines & Multivoltage				
BB 12000	S.N.C.F.	1954	148	3,600
BB 16000	S.N.C.F.	1958	62	5,540
BB 16500	S.N.C.F.	1958	294	3,600†
BB 17000	S.N.C.F.	1965	52	3,500†
CC 14100	S.N.C.F.	1954	102	2,500*
BB 25100, 25200	S.N.C.F.	1964	71	5,540‡
BB 25500	S.N.C.F.	1964	50	3,500†

* — fitted with rheostatic or regenerative braking
† — fitted with monomotor and change-speed bogies
‡ — 4,500 h.p. only on D.C.

Note: The BB 8500, 17000, and 25500 classes are identical in all respects except electrically, as are the BB 16000 and 25100 classes.

SNCF 040TA class 0–8–0T No. 040TA53, the shed pilot at Sotteville m.p.d. shunts hopper wagons of graded coal for the stoker fired engines at this depot. *[B. Stephenson*

The northbound "Mistral" about to leave Nice, with 141R.1151 at the head. In common with many of the later 141Rs, and all the final series, this machine was oil-burning; the coal-burning members of the class were however equipped with mechanical stokers. *[Dr. P. Ransome-Wallis*

Ex-P.L.M. 4-cylinder compound 4–8–4T No. 242TA.54 at Paris (Nord) *[Dr. P. Ransome-Wallis*

MISTRAL
141.R

242 TA 54
2

South Croydon, 1950.

The Oxted line since 1948

by Michael Baker

For thirty years now the Oxted line has been the last non-electrified section of the old London, Brighton & South Coast Railway in the London area, and from 1961 to 1963 it was responsible for the last scheduled steam-worked services out of Victoria station. It has therefore long been an odd man out in the Southern Electric network, and an interesting one.

Although the South Eastern Railway had proposed to build from Norwood Junction (Croydon) to Dover via Oxted and Edenbridge in 1839, they later decided instead to share the L.B. & S.C.R's route across the North Downs through the Merstham Gap, and their main line therefore commenced at Redhill. Oxted did not in the event see a railway until 1884, when the Croydon & Oxted Joint Railway was opened by both companies together. South of Oxted, at Crowhurst, the S.E.R. built a spur connecting with their main line from Redhill to Dover, but the L.B. & S.C. continued the new railway southwards to East Grinstead, and in 1888 from Hurst Green (near Oxted) to Ashurst, connecting at both places with the older Three Bridges—East Grinstead-Tunbridge Wells branch, and forming through routes to London from the recently-opened Bluebell Line (East Grinstead-Lewes) and Cuckoo Line (Eridge-Hailsham-Eastbourne). At its northern end the Croydon & Oxted joined the London to Brighton main line at South Croydon and the South Eastern's Mid-Kent branch at Woodside; but in fact the South Eastern contributed little to the business and the Oxted line settled down as a more or less integral part of the L.B. & S.C. network.

Since the line was built London has expanded vastly into the Surrey hills and there has been a great deal of development along the Sussex coastline, but between these areas and in the area the line serves, relatively little has changed. The Oxted line itself has always been reasonably busy and nowadays handles a fairly heavy commuter traffic to Croydon and London, but not comparable in volume with that on neighbouring lines; and although there was talk of electrification in the 1920s and 1930s the war put a stop to such plans. In 1948 the newly-formed British Railways had many more pressing responsibilities, so steam was clearly likely to remain on the Oxted line for some while.

I was a small boy at the time of nationalisation and used to spend many hours watching the trains on East Croydon Station. The only steam hauled ones, apart from freights and parcels trains (mainly running by night) and some of the Newhaven boat trains, were those on the Oxted line. Whilst they didn't strike me as being wildly glamorous, for often they consisted of no more than three coaches in the charge of a rather scruffy tank engine or a Maunsell 2–6–0, a type of locomotive one was just as likely to see pulling a goods train, and none of them were what you could properly call express, they were for all that steam trains amongst an almost overwhelming crowd of electrics. Although most of them terminated at East Grinstead or Tunbridge Wells a few worked right through to Eastbourne or Brighton and made it possible to travel all the way by steam to either of these Sussex resorts long after the direct route had been electrified. Of course the journey time was much greater than on the direct route, but there was considerable compensation in the delightful scenery as the titles of the Bluebell and Cuckoo lines might suggest. The rural character of the area served might lead one to suppose that the density of the population was rather low, which was indeed the case; and consequently one might expect the railway to be particularly vulnerable to competition from the motor car in the affluent post war years. Here again such a supposition would be correct, but in 1948 this competition was a threat rather than an accomplished fact and the branch line network of East Sussex was still intact.

Owing to its vast electrification programme the Southern never found it necessary to build any passenger tank engines, except for the short-lived "River" class 2–6–4Ts. The L.B. & S.C.R. had, on the other hand been much addicted to them and as the Oxted line was ideally suited to tank engine operation several Brighton classes were still to be found there at the time of nationalisation. By far the largest numerically were the I3s. Twenty-seven of them had been built between 1907 and 1913 and all but one were still in existence. They were the mainstay of the line and as well as handling many of the East Grinstead and Tunbridge Wells trains also worked through to Brighton and Eastbourne. They had been amongst the earliest engines equipped with superheaters and in their heyday had created a great stir by running the Sunny South Express non-stop from Willesden Junction to Brighton on one tankful of water. The London and North Western 4–4–0s which the I3s relieved at Willesden had been using coal and water at a rate more suitable to a small Cunarder, and Crewe, following the example of the I3s, made haste to fit superheaters to many of their passenger and goods engines. In those days the L.N.W.R. really was the Premier Line and was probably only just aware of the L.B. & S.C.R's. existence so the effect of the I3s may be imagined.

Marsh produced a lot more 4–4–2Ts, none of much account, but eighteen of one of these classes, the I1X, survived in 1948. They saw little service but occasionally one would come tottering up from Brighton or Eastbourne. The successors to the 4–4–2Ts and the largest Brighton tanks still in their original form were the two 4–6–2Ts, Nos. 2325 and 2326 which were shedded at Tunbridge Wells and frequently worked up to East Croydon and London. They had been repainted in the malachite green livery reserved for express passenger classes and were generally kept much cleaner than most Oxted line engines. There was one other ex L.B. & S.C.R. passenger tank class seen between Oxted and Croydon and that was the D3 0–4–4T, a type which mostly worked on push and pull trains on the Oxted-Tunbridge Wells line but which sometimes penetrated further north.

Turning to mixed traffic and goods engines, the 0–6–2T was a favourite wheel arrangement on the L.B. & S.C.R. and 134 of them, comprising four different classes, had been turned out by Brighton Works between 1891 and 1905. All but four, but many of them rebuilt, were taken over by British Railways; though despite the fact that they were to be seen all over the Central section, weren't particularly common on the Oxted line. Norwood Junction shed possessed a great many of the smaller wheeled variety but they were mostly employed on shunting and local pick-up freights on the South London electrified lines and seldom ventured out into the country. The larger wheeled classes were much commoner south of East Grinstead and Tunbridge Wells, but what goods traffic there was on the Oxted line was mostly in the hands of the C2X 0–6–0s. These originated between 1893 and 1902, were rebuilt with larger boilers and all forty-five passed into British Railways ownership.

Apart from the tank engines there were the ex-Brighton passenger and

The 5.40 p.m. London Bridge-Lewes at Oxted in 1951, headed by L.B. & S.C.R. H2 class Atlantic No. 32425. "Trevose Head". [Derek Cross

A northbound pick-up goods at Oxted in 1959, with C2X class 0–6–0 No. 32544. [Derek Cross

mixed traffic tender engines, smaller in numbers than the tanks but still in evidence in 1948. The most modern were L. B. Billinton's sixteen K class 2–6–0s of 1913-21. Their principal duties were heavy freight workings on the main line from Three Bridges and Brighton sheds but they put in appearances on the Oxted line from time to time on both goods and passenger trains. Of the express tender engines there were seven B4 4–4–0s, the earliest of which dated back to 1899, and twelve of the much more modern looking rebuilds, the B4X. Both classes regularly worked Oxted trains.

But the most splendid of all the Brighton engines were the Atlantics. Their designer, Douglas Earle Marsh, had come from the Great Northern Railway and in 1905 produced for the Brighton something very similar to an Ivatt large boilered 4–4–2. Four more appeared in that year and the next, and six of a slightly modified design, the H2, in 1911-12. Two of the H1s had been withdrawn during the war and a third, No. 2039 "Hartland Point", was in 1947 rebuilt with sleeve valve gear in connection with Bulleid's Leader class and never returned to regular traffic, but one of the two others, No. 2039 "Portland Bill", and all the H2s were once again resplendent in fully lined out malachite green livery, and were much in evidence on the heaviest rush hour workings, in particular the 5.40 p.m. London Bridge-Lewes, and the 6.10 p.m. Victoria-Uckfield. I have a vivid recollection of a spotless "North Foreland" overtaking the electric train in which I was travelling near Wandsworth Common, and in those days immediately after the war a clean engine really was a great novelty.

The Maunsell Moguls mentioned earlier were of the N and U1 types and were by far the most common of the Southern Railway-built engines seen on the Oxted line although a Q or Q1 would sometimes appear on a freight train in place of a pre-grouping 0–6–0.

Ex-S.E. & C.R. locomotives, despite the fact that the company had been joint owner of the Croydon and Oxted Railway were far less common than those of the L.B. & S.C.R. A Wainwright or Kirtley 0–4–4T had a regular mid-afternoon working up to East Croydon which took it back to Tunbridge Wells at the tail end of the rush hour, and from time to time a Stewarts Lane, Brighton or Tonbridge inside cylinder 4–4–0 worked through to Tunbridge Wells or Brighton. Apart from turns by C or sometimes O1 0–6–0s on freight trains that was about the extent of ex S.E. & C.R. working over the Oxted line.

The most modern class to appear, and one that was still being added to in 1948 was the Bulleid West Country/Battle of Britain 4–6–2. Two, No. 21C156 "Croydon" and 21C168 "Kenley" were named after airfields situated within a mile or so of the Oxted line, and although I personally never saw either of them working on it, it is quite possible that one or both did.

Such then was the locomotive scene in 1948. It was to change greatly in the next four years but before moving on it might be interesting to take a look at the coaching stock.

Here the South Eastern took its revenge over the Brighton for coaches of the latter company were non-existent north of Oxted, whilst the "birdcage" sets built by the former were absolutely rampant. There were also a number of post grouping corridor coaches in use, Maunsell vehicles dating from the 1920s and the early 30s.

As nationalisation set in strange things began to happen in the paint shops. Some of the Maunsell corridor coaches got themselves decked out in red and cream which was quite nice but not really "them", and the birdcage sets started to go a rather murky shade of Post Office red. Engines had "British Railways" painted on the tank or tender sides instead of "Southern", first in the same green shaded style, then in a very austere sans serif typeface, and finally lettering disappeared altogether to be replaced by the lion-balanced-on-a-monocycle emblem. A few engines carried an "S" prefix but by April, 1948 it had been decided that all Southern locomotives should have 30,000 added to their numbers. One of the very first to receive her new number was the J2 4–6–2T No. 32326, although she retained her green Southern Railway livery. Her sister engine was renumbered eleven months later in March, 1949 on emerging from Brighton works following repairs necessitated by damage sustained when she was derailed at Lewes whilst working the 1.57 p.m. from Tunbridge Wells. She too kept her green livery even though the I3s and some of the 0–6–2Ts were by then beginning to appear in lined black.

Meanwhile the I1Xs were being withdrawn and by the end of October, 1948 there were nine left; then there seemed to be something of a reprieve for there were still eight in February, 1950. The first H2 to be withdrawn was No. 2423 "The Needles" in May, 1949, but the class still regularly worked Oxted trains and also relief Newhaven boat expresses, and fears about the fate of the survivors were alleviated when all five were repainted in British Railways lined black passenger livery. It was towards the end of 1950 that the holocaust really hit the Brighton express engines.

In the summer of that year the first of the Fairburn L.M.S. type 2–6–4Ts intended for use on the Southern Region emerged from Brighton works and was sent to Tunbridge Wells shed. Another forty quickly followed, some of them for the Eastern Section, but most for the Oxted line. The effect on the ex L.B. & S.C.R. engines was immediate. In October the two 4–6–2Ts moved from Tunbridge Wells to Brighton, by Christmas there was only one I1X left, No. 2002, and in January, 1951 the last regular working by an I3 into Victoria, an Eastbourne engine on the 10.6 a.m. from Tunbridge Wells, ceased. In the middle of 1951 production of the L.M.S. type 2–6–4Ts ended at Brighton and gave way to the B.R. Standard engines of the same wheel arrangement, and a number of these also took up work on the Oxted line. The introduction of a new standard class always seemed to cause resentment in those days as well as interest, mostly I suppose because it meant the disappearance of old favourites, which was certainly the case on the Oxted line, but the big Riddles tanks were handsome machines and over the years grew to be almost as much a part of the landscape as Oxted Parish Church. By the end of 1951 the I1X, the J1 and J2, the B4 and B4X and the H1 classes had all ceased to exist. The last I3 was withdrawn on May 10th, 1952. All that then survived of the ex L.B. & S.C.R. express engine stud was the five H2s, the seven rebuilt N15Xs on the Western Section and "Gladstone" in York museum.

Whilst all this upheaval was going on in the locomotive world, the coaching scene stayed much the same. The early 1950s saw the gradual introduction of first Bulleid, and then British Railways standard corridors, but the birdcages, as well as the Maunsell stock, survived and for a while a rush hour Oxted line train was almost a history of railway carriages in South East England since the turn of the century. The Maunsell coaches never looked quite right in the red and cream livery, and when word came from—well, not On High but from someone in authority that they could go back to green if they really wanted to they all very rapidly did. The three-coach standard sets obviously felt much happier with their top halves cream and their bottoms red and some of them remained thus as late as 1962. The South Eastern coaches gradually reassumed green livery but like the standards appeared to be in no great hurry. Apart from the three-coach sets into which nearly all of them were formed, there were a few loose ones, mostly ten-compartment thirds built just before the grouping, one seven-coach set which worked the 7.8 a.m. from Tunbridge Wells West to London Bridge and returned at 5.20 p.m., and for a short while, one of the curious brake tri-composites, the only pre-1914 S.E. & C.R. vehicles with corridor connections: they had been provided for through working with vehicles from more enlightened companies north of the Thames.

For a time after 1951 the Oxted line settled down, with its variety of coaching stock and its motive power mainly the two varieties of 2–6–4T and Maunsell 2–6–0s, and then, in 1957, the equivalent of the slaughter of the Brighton express engines in 1950-51 overtook the carriages. Diesel-electric multiple units were introduced on the Hastings line and these released the flat sided, narrow bodied Maunsell corridors built for that service during the late 1920s and early 30s, for work elsewhere. A number of them came to the Oxted line and overnight it seemed practically all the South Eastern coaches vanished. A few of the later thirds were retained, appearing in twos on rush hour trains, but they were rather austere and sombre in their interior fittings compared with their older relations, whose bulbous light globes, looking as if they ought to have contained gas mantles, set into white-painted matchboarded and beamed ceilings, and the rather faded but deep cushions, were the epitome of Edwardian opulence. One half expected the guard to come in and water the aspidistra. Fortunately such delights may still be sampled at Sheffield Park where some splendid examples graze contentedly on the Bluebell Line. The Maunsell Corridors, too, had rather nice interiors but one had to be careful about getting out of them on the corridor side: although there was a droplight between each large window, only every other one was actually a door, a feature which at some of the brisk stops on the Oxted line could lead to incidents calculated to shorten the lives of old ladies by at least five years. Perhaps Mr. Maunsell witnessed such a happening for doors without handles were a feature he abandoned on his later coaches. The South Eastern seven-coach set was replaced by one of similar length containing a type of vehicle never very common on non-electric trains on any part of the Southern

Region, and unique to the Central section. This was that once numerous but very short-lived creature, the B.R. Standard non-corridor coach. The set contained five of them, originally painted red and later green, and two Bulleid corridor firsts.

It was also in 1957 that the last of the Standard class "4" tanks, No. 80154, emerged from Brighton works. It was put to work on the Oxted line which by then was almost exclusively worked by 2–6–4Ts. Almost, but not quite; for Maunsell and Billinton 2–6–0s, Bulleid Pacifics, and ex South Eastern Hs and 4–4–0s still appeared, and on summer Saturdays, when the larger engines were off working holiday extras C, Q and Q1 0–6–0s were promoted to passenger duty: which, with all the commuters down at the golf club or at home mowing their lawns, was much lighter than during the week. Tunbridge Wells shed possessed at this time some Ivatt 2–6–2Ts and these sometimes worked up to London, although it was my experience that they were hard put to keep time with anything more than three coaches.

Apart from a short visit from the experimental Fell diesel-mechanical 4–8–4 the Oxted line was still entirely steam operated but dieselisation and electrification on the Eastern section from 1957 onwards had a considerable effect upon it. The transfer of the Hastings line coaches has already been mentioned, but the end of steam working there had another consequence and that was the redundancy of the Schools class 4–4–0s shedded at St. Leonards. These had always done a limited amount of work on the Central Section but now a number of them were shedded at Brighton and soon took up regular duties on the Oxted line. No. 30901 "Winchester" was a particularly consistent performer on the 7.19 a.m. Brighton to London Bridge and the return working at 4.40 p.m.

A new class, indeed a new wheel arrangement to the Oxted line, the standard "4" 4–6–0 appeared early in 1959. It may seem odd that no sort of 4–6–0 had ever regularly worked the route before, but neither the L.B. & S.C.R. nor the South Eastern possessed any and I have no knowledge of any of the Maunsell varieties appearing. The year before the introduction of the 4–6–0s a wheel arrangement once familiar on the Oxted line had disappeared, not just from the central section of the Southern, but from British Railways entirely. The last Brighton Atlantic, No. 32424 "Beachy Head", made its final run on Sunday, 13th April, 1958 working a replica continental express from Victoria to Newhaven. The class had been little seen on the Oxted line in their last years, living in semi-retirement at Brighton emerging at Christmas to work parcels traffic, and at summer weekends holiday expresses over the route where the I3s had first achieved fame in the years before the First World War. Another Brighton class, the D3 0–4–4T, had become extinct at the end of 1955, the last survivor, No. 32390, working Oxted to East Croydon trains for a number of weeks immediately before withdrawal. The next class to disappear was, surprisingly, the Fairburn 2–6–4Ts, not for scrapping, but in exchange for a similar number of standard "4" tanks from the L.M.R. This meant that there were really an awful lot of these engines at work on the Oxted line but still not so many that ex-L.B. & S.C.R. engines were completely excluded.

The first part of the Kent Coast electrification came into operation on the 14th June, 1959 and two years later almost to the day the whole scheme was completed. A great many locomotives consequently found themselves out of work, and were either scrapped or transferred to the Central or Western sections. Amongst the carriages which moved over to the Oxted line were some very handsome Maunsell Corridors of a profile almost identical to that of the Portsmouth line express electric stock trailer cars, and two three-sets of them were employed on the East Grinstead train in which Dr. Beeching used to travel in the summer of 1961 when he was head of British Railways. By now many of the older Maunsell coaches were being withdrawn although some of the S.E. & C.R. seconds lasted into 1962.

A number of rebuilt West Country/Battle of Britain Pacifics from Eastern section sheds were regularly diagrammed over the Oxted line in 1961. No.

34100 "Appledore", in immaculate condition after working the Golden Arrow during the last weeks of steam operation was one such engine which was often on the 2.02 p.m. from Brighton to Victoria.

The greater part of this train consisted of vans containing thousands of boxes of flowers from the Sussex nurseries which, as I was spending the summer holidays working as a porter at Victoria, it was often my job to help unload. They arrived as the evening rush hour was approaching and as platform space was consequently at a premium, when all the passengers had alighted the train was shunted out to allow the engine to escape and the vans were then propelled back up to the buffers, which left enough room for an empty suburban electric to come up behind. The moment the van doors were opened a cascade of flowerboxes would be propelled at fearful speed across the platform in an effort to get finished in time for us to rush across to the Eastern side of the station and maybe remove ten shillings from an unwary American off one of the boat trains. I fear we paid scant regard for the lives of the commuters and there must be many a citizen of Epsom who wondered what he'd done to warrant a clout round the ear from a box of prize blooms as he picked his perilous way down platform 16. At that time an army of students used to descend on Victoria each June eager to earn a fortune in eight weeks, we tried to survive on this until we all became postmen for ten days at Christmas. We came from all over the country and Eire too, and though we were willing and eager were liable to commit from time to time such youthful indiscretions as leaving doors open on trains departing from platform 10 and having them knocked off by the Golden Arrow, so that eventually British Railways learnt the error of their ways and decided that most of us would do less harm if we went back to assisting Irish gentlemen on building sites or marking examination papers.

I spent July and August of that year and the next at Victoria and consequently had a unique opportunity of watching the London end of the Oxted line at work. There were, of course a number of trains which ran from London Bridge, particularly during the rush hours, but the service was mostly concentrated on Victoria. Although other classes appeared, a very great proportion, over 80%, were by then hauled by the standard "4" tanks. However, one very interesting engine appeared briefly in June, 1961, and that was D1 class 4–4–0 No. 31739. I had travelled behind her on the 7.24 a.m. from London Bridge to Ramsgate via Sevenoaks and Tonbridge a few days before the end of steam operation to the Kent coast, and in the following week she appeared on the Oxted line on the 4.40 p.m. from London Bridge to Brighton. I saw her again on June 19th, but by August the train was in the charge of a Schools and as far as I know 31739 was the last of the long line of Stirling, Wainwright and Maunsell inside cylinder 4–4–0s to work on the Oxted route. The days of the still surviving D1s, E1s, Ls and L1s were by the summer of 1961 very definitely numbered and in July most of them were in store at Nine Elms shed awaiting their final journey to the breakers yard.

At Victoria there were still occasional appearances by pre-grouping engines, Ns, N1s and once a C2X, No. 32539 on empty stock for an evening Tunbridge Wells train. A rather suprising visitor on at least two occasions was one of the then recently formed auto-trains made up of a Maunsell open second and a brake composite. It had strayed up from its usual haunts between Oxted and Tunbridge Wells and wasn't of course worked as a push and pull on its excursions up to the bright lights, being hauled each time (another oddity) by a Q 0–6–0.

The eastern side of Victoria station had gone completely electric apart from a type "3" diesel on the Golden Arrow and Night Ferry empty stock and just one steam engine, an H 0–4–4T which used to indulge in a little light shunting. To be strictly accurate, the Eastern side did still see some steam hauled passenger trains but these were off the Oxted line and were switched across from the Brighton side at the bottom of Grosvenor Bridge into platform seven. They were the Lingfield race specials and with pullman cars in their nine, ten or eleven coach

The Bluebell Railway's ex-L&SWR Adams 4–4–2T, once BR No. 30583, at Sheffield Park: also visible are the ex-GWR "Dukedog" 4–4–0 No. 9017 and an ex-SE&CR "P" class 0–6–0T. [*J. B. Snell*

Ex-GNR 0–6–0T No. 1247, LNER class J52, at Haworth on the Keighley & Worth Valley Railway. [*B. A. Seaton*

Scottish Malt Distillers Ltd; the Balmenach Distillery Barclay 0–4–0T, built in 1937, at Cromdale in 1967.
[*J. M. Boyes*

British Aluminium Company; Peckett 0–4–0T No. 1 at Burntisland (Fife) in 1967. Privately-owned industrial steam locomotives like these two will remain in service for some years yet, outside the preservation movement.
[*D. Cross*

The Oxted-Tonbridge locals used to produce a wide variety of locomotives, though they were usually very light trains. E4 0–6–2T No. 32581 leaves Oxted bunker-first.

Ex-South Eastern engines predominated on the line. Here H class 0–4–4T No. 31544 crosses the viaduct at Oxted.

D1 4–4–0 No. 31489 emerges from a cutting near Hever.

C class 0–6–0 No. 31280 leaves Hever station for Oxted. All this set of photographs were taken in 1960. [*Derek Cross*

make up were the nearest thing the Oxted line ever got to an express. They were headed by standard "4" 4–6–0s and Maunsell Moguls. One of the former engines from Three Bridges also appeared at Victoria on the 8.20 a.m. from Forest Row and went out again at 3.50 p.m. Occasionally a U1 would substitute, but whichever class was in charge the train was always made up of exactly the right number of coaches to permit the engine to stand level with the porters' hut on platform sixteen, and it would while away the time until departure by blowing off steam with great enthusiasm which in the confines of Victoria station was nearly enough to burst ones eardrums. We grew heartily sick of nasty, noisy steam engines and there were certain afternoons when we should have been most happy to have exchanged the lot for quiet, well behaved diesels.

I don't really suppose there was any connection, but in the spring of 1962 our wish began to come true: the 3-car diesel-electric units which had long been promised for the Oxted line began to appear. By the middle of that summer there were a dozen or so in service and a consequent reduction in the number and variety of steam workings. The "Schools" and the pre-grouping engines, apart from an occasional N, had gone, leaving all the remaining steam trains in the hands of the standard "4" tanks and a few standard 4–6–0s and light Pacifics, which latter also once in a while substituted for an electric locomotive on the Newhaven boat train. The locomotive-hauled coaching stock had been decimated too, the last of the S.E. & C.R. vehicles had gone, and although there were still a number of Maunsells in use, in particular the Hastings variety, a great many had been withdrawn and were stored on the down line of the Haywards Heath to Horsted Keynes branch awaiting breaking up at Lancing Works.

The summer of 1962 was the last one to see steam locomotives in any numbers at Victoria. More diesel-electric sets came into use in the autumn and at the end of the 1963 summer timetable diagrammed steam working on the Oxted line ceased.

K class 2–6–0 No. 32343 at Birchden Junction with a Tunbridge Wells-Brighton goods.
[*Derek Cross*

Certain Brighton via Oxted trains used to divide at Ashurst, the rear half going to Tunbridge Wells. Here 3-cylinder U1 2–6–0 No. 31908 leaves for Brighton, with Maunsell Q 0–6–0 No. 30538 waiting to take on the remainder. [*Derek Cross*

Q class 0–6–0 No. 30533 on a Victoria-Tunbridge Wells train passing the junction with the line from East Grinstead and Three Bridges, south of Ashurst. [*Derek Cross*

C class No. 31695, on a goods from the Cuckoo Line, passing some characteristic Kentish architecture near Eridge. [*Derek Cross*

"Schools" class 4–4–0 No. 30918 "Hurstpierpoint" on a London Bridge-Brighton train entering Ashurst, passing a C2X 0–6–0. [Derek Cross

The standard tanks, the 4–6–0s and the Pacifics moved over to the Western section as did the Bulleid coaches. Nearly all the remaining Maunsells were withdrawn, although some worked for another few months on the Tonbridge-Redhill-Reading line. The standard coaches remained as there were still some locomotive-hauled workings, now in the charge of Birmingham-Sulzer type 3 diesels. A number of B.R. standard loco-hauled coaches were drafted in as well, some from other regions and still in red livery. They are still there, now painted blue and grey, and work between Brighton and Victoria and on certain East Grinstead rush-hour trains. The variety of coaching stock hasn't quite vanished, as there is a most peculiar rush-hour train, the 17.20 London Bridge-Crowborough, made up of ex 4-SUB electric stock trailers with a BIL motor coach at each end minus power equipment but still with driving compartment, the whole ensemble hauled by a Type 3 diesel.

The complexities of the Oxted line workings have been much simplified over the years owing to the closure of a large part of the network. The Bluebell Line between Lewes and East Grinstead finally expired in 1958, then the Cuckoo Line from Eridge as far as Hailsham was closed in 1965; consequently it was no longer possible to travel from London to Eastbourne via Oxted. At the beginning of 1967 the Three Bridges-East Grinstead-Tunbridge Wells service ceased. There are now no through trains from Tunbridge Wells West to Oxted and London, and almost the only trains that serve the West station are those from Eridge to Tonbridge. These too are threatened, together with those from Oxted to Eridge and Lewes. This would leave no service via Oxted except the London-East Grinstead trains; but for the sake of their commuter business they seem likely to last. But it is hardly conceivable that the line will be electrified, so that it will remain the Southern's odd-man-out in the London area.

Whyteleafe, 1960. ["*Drawings by the Author*"

From the Archives

FIFTY YEARS AGO

Top: North Stafford Railway: an express for Manchester leaving Stoke-on-Trent, with 4–4–0 No. 87.

Centre: Caledonian Railway: a local train arriving at Carlisle, with "Dunalastair II" 4–4–0 No. 772.

Bottom: Maryport & Carlisle Railway: train leaving Carlisle, with 0–4–2 No. 4.
[Loco. Pub. Co.

CREWS AND CHARGES

Upper: G.W.R. broad gauge Gooch 4–2–2 X 'Timour' at Newton Abbot, 1886.
[*British Railways*

Lower: Union Pacific RR; 4–6–0 No. 915 at Denver in 1900.
[*R. H. Kindig coll.*

STEAM AND STATIONS

Upper: Florence station in the 1850s, with an artist's impression of a 2–2–2 drawn with somewhat less eye for detail than the architecture. [*Italian State Railways*

Lower: Liverpool (Lime Street) over a century later, with a Caprotti-valve B.R. standard class 5 4–6–0. [*P. Gerald*

4–8–2 No. 704, built at Montreal in 1947, on freight near Machava. [*A. E. Durrant*

The Railways of Moçambique and their locomotives

by A. E. Durrant

Although much has been written about the neighbouring South African and Rhodesian railway systems, surprisingly little has been published about the interesting network in Portuguese East Africa. A glance at the map will show that this system is characterised both by its lack of continuity and by its abundance of international connections, with no fewer than four other states (Malawi, Rhodesia, South Africa, and Swaziland) having rail outlets via Moçambique ports.

The most important section of the Caminhos de Ferro Moçambique (C.F.M.) runs inland from Lourenco Marques and was originally commenced about 1887 as the Delagoa Bay Railway, linking the Transvaal Republic at Komatipoort with the Indian Ocean. Some financial troubles not unconnected with bad management led to the withdrawal of the original American concession in June 1883 and the reformation of the line as the C.F. Lourenco Marques under the Moçambique government.

Today this busy division, which includes extensive harbour installations, has a double track main line as far as Machava, 6 miles out; from which junction, the focal point of the system, branches diverge to the important secondary port of Matola and also to the Swaziland border at Goba. The main line continues to Ressano Garcia, the frontier station with South Africa, whilst the Rhodesian main line, which diverges at Oficina Gerais on the outskirts of Lourenco Marques, heads north to Malvernia, following the Limpopo River for much of its distance.

From Goba the Swaziland Railway commences. This is a line opened only in 1964, which exists primarily for the transportation of iron ore from the mines near Mbabane to Matola, whence it is shipped to Japan. The S.R. forms an integral part of the C.F.M., since without the latter it would cease to function, having no ocean terminal and also no motive power of its own; all this is provided by the C.F.M. It will be interesting to see what happens when Swaziland gains its independence in September 1968, and whether commonsense will prevail over nationalism in the running of its railway, the two outlooks being incompatible.

Heading north up the coast, one meets two disconnected lines of a purely local character. The first, starting at João Belo, is of 75 cm. gauge, the only section of the C.F.M. not of the standard southern African 3′ 6″ gauge, and was rhapsodised over by C.S. Small in his book "Far Wheels". Next is the line from Inhambane to Inharrime, which meanders more or less from nowhere to nowhere, and exists mainly for passenger traffic.

The fourth line up is the next most important after the Lourenco Marques division, and also the next oldest, having begun as a 2′ 0″ gauge concern in the 1890s. As such, it penetrated through to Umtali. However, the traffic offering soon outgrew the narrow gauge and it was converted to 3′ 6″, the first section being widened as early as 1900, only two years after it had been opened! As a 3′ 6″ gauge line, it was known as the Beira, Mashonaland, and Rhodesia Railway, and was worked by the Rhodesia Railways for some time. However, since 1945 the section in Portuguese East Africa has been sold to the C.F.M., together with the locomotives operating on it. This line is by far the most severely graded of all those in Moçambique, and is worked entirely by Garratt locomotives; all the C.F.M. Garratts are allocated to it.

From Dondo, 29 km. from Beira, runs what used to be the Trans-Zambesia Railway, as far as the banks of that river at Muracca. From there, a ferry connection was made with the Central African Railway into Nyasaland. The T.Z.R. and the C.A.R. were under common management and had identical equipment and rolling stock. The Zambesi has now been bridged, and, over the border, the C.A.R. inside the former Nyasaland has become the Malawi Railway. The T.Z.R. remained independent until 1967, when it was purchased by the C.F.M., and it now forms part of the through route to the coalfields at Tete, this having previously been served by the Caminho de Ferro Tete, which formed a branch of the T.Z.R.

The fifth railway up the coast runs inland from Quelimane, and this was for a long time thought to be meter-gauge. However, examination of some Quelimane diagrams has shown that the distance of 1 metre is given between the tyres of the wheels, so that the actual track gauge will be the standard 3′ 6″. This line is of purely local character.

The northernmost line in Moçambique is also the most recent, having been commenced as recently as 1944. Starting from the port of Nacala, this line is still being extended towards the shores of Lake Malawi; at its coastal end it has a branch to Lumbo, opposite Moçambique Island.

Like most railways in southern Africa, the C.F.M. exists mainly for freight haulage, and passenger trains are both slow and infrequent; branch trains are generally mixed. The busiest service is from Lourenco Marques to Ressano Garcia, boasting five trains daily each way, one of which is the international "express" to Pretoria and Johannesburg; this actually stops at all stations (bar one) until it reaches Nelspruit, 127 miles, after which it does become an express. There is also a twice-weekly through train from Lourenco Marques to Bulawayo and back, but no service to Swaziland, since the Swaziland Railway is a freight-only concern; passenger services terminate at Goba, to which point they run twice daily.

Possibly the last class of Atlantics in regular service in the world are the Henschel-built ones in service on the Northern Line: No. 812 on a light passenger train. [*C. E. Rickwood*

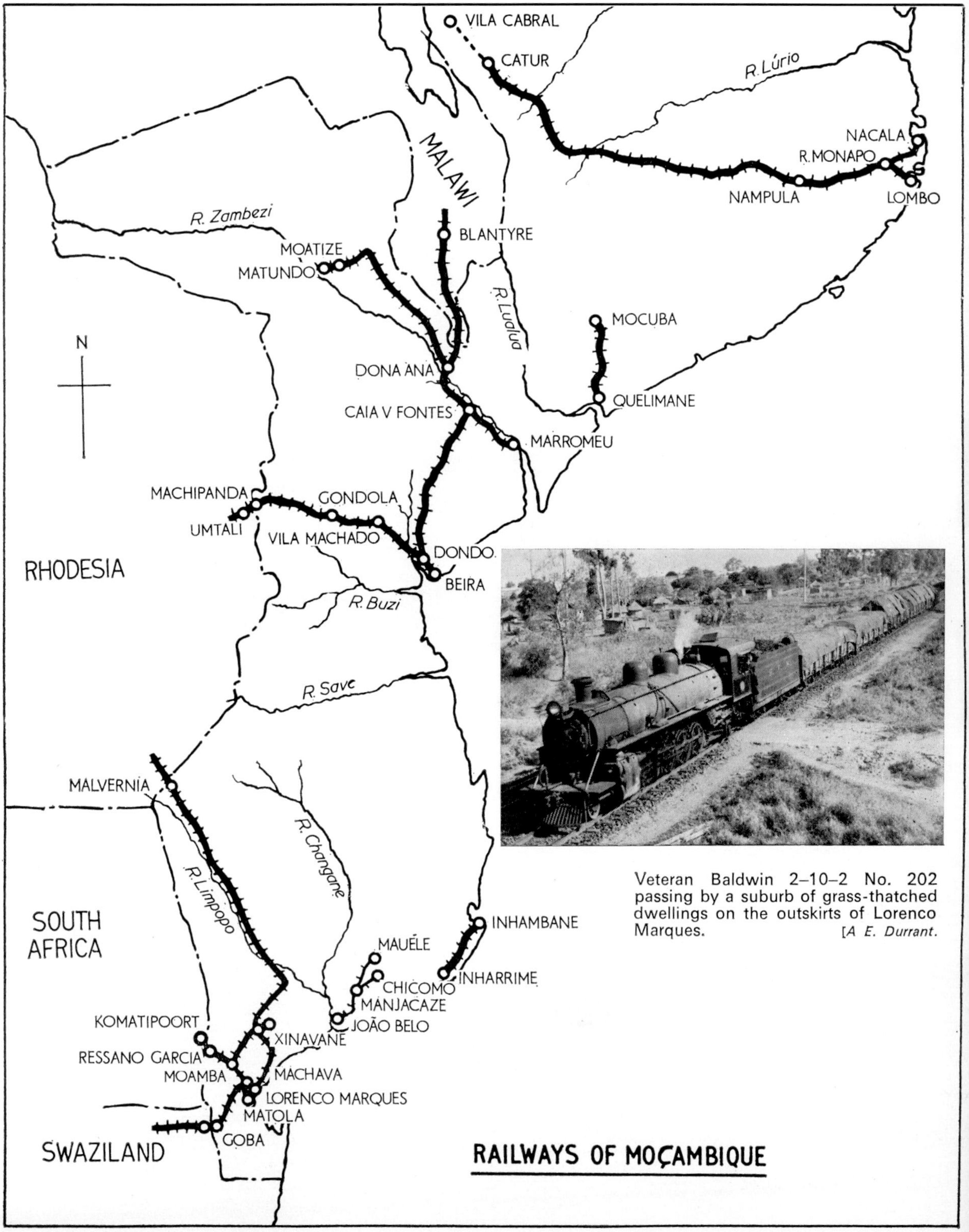

Veteran Baldwin 2–10–2 No. 202 passing by a suburb of grass-thatched dwellings on the outskirts of Lorenco Marques. [A E. Durrant.

Pacific No. 304 on a local train at Lourenco Marques. [*J. D. Blyth*

Baldwin-built 75-cm gauge 2–8–0 No. 6 of the Joao Belo line. [*Frank Jux*

4–6–4+4–6–4 Beyer-Garratt No. 927, originally built for the Sudan Railways and later in service in Rhodesia, at Beira. [*C. E. Rickwood*

A further international service runs to Limbe, with a connection to Blantyre; a daily train has 3rd and 4th class, with a twice-weekly first and second class railcar as well. A further service runs from Beira, daily, to Salisbury. Branch lines and other local services range from twice weekly to daily, the Quelimane train running daily but at a different time each day!

As might be expected from such a system as the C.F.M., the locomotives are of great variety; the stock of 218 steam locomotives includes 30 different classes, not counting the 3 varieties represented among the 7 75 cm. gauge engines.

The oldest locomotives in service are five 0–6–4Ts, survivors of 30 purchased from South Africa for working the original C.F.L.M. These have long since been replaced by more modern power, and dispersed among the northern divisions. An even older locomotive is preserved at Lourenco Marques shed, a 4–6–0T built by Dübs in 1891 for the Delagoa Bay Railway, and withdrawn from active service in 1934.

Both the Imhambane and Quelimane sections depend mainly upon a few light 2–8–0s for their haulage, supplemented in the case of the latter by two of the later Baldwin 2–8–2s, while shunting is performed by the old 0–6–4Ts. All locomotives on these two sections burn wood, as opposed to the coal used elsewhere.

Traffic after the first World War seems to have boomed, as the American firm of Baldwin received orders for power to replace the old 0–6–4Ts as main line engines. They then built 5 Pacifics, 4 2–8–2s, and 10 2–10–2s, all delivered between 1915 and 1924. These were all thoroughly American types, and an article in the house magazine "Baldwin Locomotives" for October 1925 seems to have been the first serious account of Moçambique railways.

Henschel of Kassel were the next builders favoured, and between 1925 and 1938 they delivered 4 Atlantics for passenger service, 8 2–8–2s for freight, 8 2–6–2s for mixed traffic and 9 0-10-0T heavy shunters.

There was the inevitable gap due to the second war, after which Baldwin were again in first with 10 2–8–2s and 3 2–10–2s to their previous designs, plus 6 2–8–2Ts, whilst the Montreal Locomotive Works contributed 8 large 4–8–2s based upon the South African Railways' 15F design. Thereafter Henschel got some more orders, supplying 9 0–8–2Ts, 4 2–8–2Ts, 28 2–10–2s, 2 2–8–2s and 3 Pacifics. Additionally, they built five large 4–8–2+2–8–4 Garratts. All these engines were delivered between 1950 and 1956. The Pacifics, 2–10–2s and Garratts all had mechanical stokers, and the Garratts have the distinction of being not only the last new steam locomotives built for the C.F.M. but also of being the only class to be painted in maroon instead of the usual black livery.

During the 1950s, Haine St Pierre of Belgium also delivered 12 4–8–2+2–8–4 Garratts, of the same design as those they supplied to the Bas Congo-Katanga Railway.

However, further steam power has been obtained secondhand by the C.F.M. since 1956; four GF class Garratts from the South African Railways, a number of engines from Rhodesia, mostly in the same package as the Beira-Umtali line, but including some additional power obtained to assist in working the Swaziland Railway. The former were Garratts, the latter 4–8–2s. There is some mystery as to exactly how many of these exist, two official C.F.M. sources differing as to the engine numbers, while the author has a clear photograph of a locomotive included in neither list!

When the French Congo-Ocean Railway dieselized fully in 1956, it had a number of modern locomotives for disposal, including 2–8–2s and Garratts, and the C.F.M. purchased some of each; the Garratts were of the wartime W.D. design and identical to some machines obtained from Rhodesia.

Although not strictly within the scope of this article, two derelict locomotives of more than usual interest exist at Moatize on the Tete line; these are 2–6–6–0 Mallets built by the American Locomotive Co. in 1912. Divorced from their tenders, they now act as buffer stops.

The 75-cm. gauge locomotives at João Belo are all of American build, and are of three wheel arrangements; 0–6–2, 2–6–0 and 2–8–0.

Dieselization has recently reared its ugly head with a few pilot orders placed with Japanese, German, and American builders, but with their usual tendency to break down, they have not yet become a nuisance to the steam enthusiast. In theory, the line from Lourenco Marques to Rhodesia is fully dieselized, as is the daily train to Johannesburg; but on the author's last visit, two out of four trains on the Bulawayo line were steam and four out of six S.A. "expresses" were handled by Pacifics. A tender is now out for 22 diesel railcars, to supplement the existing few, and when delivered these will doubtless spell the end for such purely passenger engines as the Baldwin 4–6–2s and the Henschel 4–4–2s. However, in common with most railways in Africa, diesels often simply take care of the additional traffic, since business is growing to such an extent that only the oldest steam engines can be scrapped; the remainder being redeployed to other parts of the system. So the visitor to Moçambique will find plenty to occupy him steamwise for a number of years to come.

The C.F.M. authorities are most helpful, and permits are readily obtainable for visiting their installations. However, these permits are necessary, especially around port areas such as Lorenco Marques and Beira, as with the current political situation, the police are liable to be rather suspicious of foreigners with cameras, and some of the northern territory is out of bounds due to the war being carried on between the defence forces and Tanzanian terrorists.

In preparing this article, the author is indebted to Messrs C. E. Rickwood, G. S. Moore, and A. H. Spit for the free use of their lists and records, and also for the use of photographs. A table of C.F.M. locomotive classes is given below.

Numbers	*Type*	*Builder*	*Date*	*Remarks*
3–5	2–8–0	Henschel	1930	
6–8	2–8–0	St. Leonard	1922	
9	4–6–0T	Dübs	1891	Preserved
10–12	4–8–0	North British	1903	Ex Rhodesia
20	2–8–0	Orenstein & Koppel	1930	
26, 34, 37, 41, 42	0–6–4T	Esslingen	1892	
50–59	0–8–2T	Henschel	1950	
61-69	0–10–0T	Henschel	1931	
81–84	2–8–2T	Henschel	1955	
91–96	2–8–2T	Baldwin	1946	
141–48	2–8–2	Societe Alsacienne	1951	Ex Congo-Ocean
200–12, 14–19	2–10–2	Baldwin	1915, 1947	
251–72	2–10–2	Henschel	1955	
301–05	4–6–2	Baldwin	1919	
331–33	4–6–2	Henschel	1955	
401–14	2–8–2	Baldwin	1924	
415–16	2–8–2	Henschel	1955	
441–46	4–8–2	?	?	Ex Rhodesia
451–59	4–8–2	Montreal	1947	Ex Rhodesia
470–79, 92	4–8–2	Bulawayo	1953	Ex Rhodesia
501–06, 11, 12	2–6–2	Henschel	1935	
571–72	2–6–2	H. K. Porter	1941	
611–16	2–8–2	Henschel	1925	
701–08	4–8–2	Montreal	1947	
811–14	4–4–2	Henschel	1925	
901–08	2–6–2+2–6–2	Beyer Peacock	1928	Ex Rhodesia
912–14	4–6–2+2–6–4	Henschel, Hanomag, Maffei	1927	Ex South Africa
921–30	4–6–4+4–6–4	Beyer Peacock	1937	Ex Sudan and Rhodesia
951–62	4–8–2+2–8–4	Haine St. Pierre	1952	
971–75	4–8–2+2–8–4	Henschel	1951	
981–89, 90–92	2–8–2+2–8–2	Beyer Peacock	1943	Ex Rhodesia OR Congo-Ocean
05	0–6–2	Baldwin	1928	75 cm gauge
06	2–8–0	Baldwin	1925	75 cm gauge
012–13	2–6–0	Alco	1919	75 cm gauge
081–83	2–8–0	Alco	1916	75 cm gauge

The Last of B.R. Steam

Above: A B.R. Class 4 4–6–0, running light engine towards the south, at Lambrigg Crossing; November 1967. [*R. I. Vallance*

Previous page: "Britannia" No. 70048 near Ais Gill with southbound freight, in March 1967. [*Paul Claxton*

Right upper: 9F 2–10–0 No. 92167 in Birkenhead Docks. [*R. I. Vallance*

Right lower. No. 92017 on a north-bound freight near Grayrigg. [*J. H. Cooper-Smith*

CANNING STREET
NORTH

92017

SHAP FINALE

This page: "Britannia" No. 70013 and B.R. Standard 4–6–0 No. 75037 hauling and banking a Preston-Carlisle freight on December 28th, 1967. Above, near Greenholme, viewed from above Scout Green; below, on the reverse curve below Scout Green. [*J. R. P. Hunt, Ian Krause*

Opposite: Above, "Britannia" No. 70024 on a northbound freight at Greenholme in October 1967, banked by a B.R. class 4 4–6–0; *below*, Fairburn 2–6–4T No. 42210 banking at Shap Wells. [*Patrick Russell, John Clarke*

Above: "Jubilee" 4–6–0 No. 45593 'Kolhapur' (now preserved) nearing Ais Gill summit with a Carlisle-Tinsley freight in May 1967.
[*Paul Claxton*

Ivatt 4MT 2–6–0 No. 43040 entering Kingmoor yard, Carlisle, with a parcels train ; November 1965.

"Britannia" 4–6–2 No. 70005 near Kingmoor with the 9.25 Crewe-Perth in November, 1965.

[*Peter J. Robinson*

Working at a Steam Shed

by O. H. Prosser

A 'Super D' in full cry: an ex-L.N.W.R. 0–8–0 on a down empty mineral train near Kenton.
[*H. Gordon Tidey*

Every sphere of human activity builds up its own heritage; certain aspects of the era of steam operation of the British railway system must be amongst the best documented facets of national life. With a full, buoyant and never ending flow of magazines and books devoted to the subject, there is much about the railways that has been reported as fully as anyone could wish. Learned histories deal with every opening and closure: periodicals announce the scrapping and putting into service of locomotives, and reference books tell of their whereabouts at given times; passenger train timing is carried out meticulously; and a thousand little sidelights receive brief mention.

In general, however, it is the information which may be amassed by the diligent onlooker or research worker which is most likely to be permanently recorded whilst that which reposes in the personal memories of a railwayman is all too often lost for ever with the passage of time. This thought occurred to me on a recent journey past the gaunt and empty rail-less shell of Aston Motive Power Depot, Birmingham, which was a brisk and bustling place when it was L.M.S. shed 3D and I did nearly a year's work there in 1946-47.

Not long after finishing war service in the Navy, I decided to answer one of the advertisements then frequently appealing in the local press for recruits to train as firemen. The serious post-war staff shortage had upset the bygone system in which the railways were able to insist on juveniles only and to pick and choose new entrants. The age limits were now sixteen to twenty five and physical fitness the only qualification stated. It was an easy job to get at that time, the establishment of cleaners and firemen was well below strength all the time I was at Aston.

My diary shows that when I began on the 12th August, 1946, it was to do a week on a duty imposed by one of the frequent coal crises of those times. Supplies from the Cannock Chase mines were falling short and all seven cleaners had to spend the day shovelling coal from reserve stocks on the ground into twelve ton trucks so that they might be raised on the coaling plant and replenish the bunker. This was hardly an inspiring opening, and neither was the next week's task. The coal shortage having apparently eased, we were bidden clean on all Aston-based engines the numbers and initials "L.M.S." The foreman cleaner was emphatic that we should not touch any visiting engines; it would have to be done, if at all, at their home sheds. It was not, of course, a satisfying job. To clean an engine properly, and see it emerge spotless and gleaming, can be a rewarding achievement, especially if one likes locomotives. To rub on

"George V" class 4–4–0 No. 25376 "Snipe" leaving Wavertree with an up parcels train in 1946.
[*Eric Treacy*

Plenty of room for oil drums on the front: Fowler 'Crab' 2-6-0 No. 13174 in LMS days [*Loco Pub. Co.*

Fowler 2–6–4T No. 2300. [*Loco Pub. Co.*

Station pilot at Birmingham (New St.) in 1938: Webb 'coal tank' 0–6–2T No. 6786.
[*L. Hanson*

enough paraffin to make number and initials legible whilst the remainder stays rusty and grimy is too much of a makeshift to please anyone. Added to the rudimentary cleaning were odd jobs like unloading firelighting wood from a truck, rolling barrels of oil into the store and hoisting them into position with a Weston purchase, and going down from the shed to Aston Station on Fowler 2–6–0 No. 2877 with stores for despatch to Crewe carried on the front. There was plenty of room in front of the smokebox on the "Crabs", no doubt why one was chosen. One could not have got much behind the buffer beam of, say an L.N.W.R. 0–8–0.

The next few weeks offered much variety, or rather variations on a theme, for shovelling came into most of them. There was sand to be put in a wheelbarrow and taken round for filling the engine boxes, ash and clinker to be moved from the disposal pits, and coal transported to where needed for lighting up. Even on one occasion sweeping out the pay offices and cleaning the baths in the enginemen's hostel fell to the lot of new cleaners. The better wages and conditions offered elsewhere had begun to cause resignations and when one of our storekeepers left I had a spell in the oil stores, issuing the right types and quantities of lubricant for the class of engine and the work it was to do. Superheated locomotives needed a heavier grade of oil for cylinder lubrication.

Stores duties introduced me to shift working, for oil had to be available at all times. Shifts continued with a transfer to what was certainly the most onerous and demanding task I did at Aston, steam raising on the engines in the shed. A steam raiser has to maintain the fires and water levels on all the engines needed for duty and the difficulty of doing this varied with the time of day and day of the week. During daylight one could get round pretty comfortably and ensure that everything was in order. At night, however, and especially on Sunday night when there were more engines in than at other times, the job became almost a nightmare. With most of our stock of 47 engines to be got ready to go out at various times after midnight, it meant going round continuously without any break, climbing up into cabs to put on the injector to fill the boiler, and building up the fire whilst the water was running. If all the injectors had taken up first time, it would not have been so bad, but some were hard to start when steam pressure was low, as of course it usually was, Some injectors would not work at all till one had built up more pressure, and when this had to be done with the water in the gauge glass low and still falling, while other engines in the shed needed attention, it became a most worrying and distracting job. One was terrified all the time of "dropping a plug"—letting the water level fall so far that the top of the firebox became uncovered and so causing the fusible lead plug to melt with risk of hundreds of pounds worth of damage. It was a fault of bad organization—of which the old L.M.S. was not free—that led to one inexperienced person being given so responsible a duty. A fireman on a train may sometimes have to work hard, but I do not think his task anything like as bad as that of a steam raiser under stress. It is far easier to concentrate on one engine than on several dozen.

From steam raising I went on to the "Disposal Link", a job we were told was done on the old Great Western by special men separate from the regular drivers and firemen. At Aston we stood by to take over engines as they arrived at the shed after road service and to prepare them either for their next turn or for repairs or boiler cleaning. The water and coal supplies had to be replenished and the smokebox and fire and ashpan cleaned. Disposing engines was essentially something to do on a calm day, when you could shovel out soot from the smokebox without getting too dirty. With a breeze, soot blew up and the disposer finished looking like a sweep. Wind also made it unpleasant when going down into the pit below the engine to pull out the ash and clinker with a long rake. The driver would lift up two or three firebars in the grate and push the clinker down into the ashpan, from which it had to be pulled out. The accessibility of the ashpan varied widely according to the engine's ground clearance, which was dictated by the size of wheel. Anything from Fowler 0–6–0s upwards was easy to do; ashpans on Webb 0–8–0s and 0–6–2 coal tanks were difficult to get at.

The first thing necessary was, of course, that the driver raise the front damper to the ashpan so that the rake could be put in. and a difficulty arose here when on one occasion No. 6004, the last "Claughton", which surprisingly outlasted all the others by some years, came down from Edge Hill. I went below and waited for the damper to be lifted, but after a few minutes the driver called out to ask me whether I knew where the control handle was in the cab. Never having been on a "Claughton" before, naturally I did not. He then said that as an old North Western man he must have had to deal with them before, but it was so long ago that he had forgotten and there was certainly no fitting like that on our own North Western engines for this purpose. He said all he could do was move every single fitting in the cab till the door came up, when I could shout and tell him it had happened. This he did and eventually lighted on the right lever; it was certainly non-standard both in position and in the fact that it moved the door by means of a ratchet allowing very nice adjustments of air supply to the grate.

Before we began that job, I had been caught for it by an adaptation of the sergeant major's means of getting "volunteers" to move the regimental piano. Mr. Harold Roberts, the Running Shift Foreman, had come into our room and said, "You're interested in engines, ar'nt you?" I had to agree, so he replied, "Well, the last 'Claughton' is on the shed; you and your mate can go and dispose it". The only other real rarity that I saw at Aston was one of the last four "George V" class 4–4–0s; I think they were all shedded at Stafford at that time. Otherwise, when I started on my first firing turns it was on designs which had in most cases been familiar since my schooldays and which nobody realized then would in a few short years be rendered extinct.

First, however, we had to go to Bescot for a week of lessons by the local firing instructor, a Mr. Jack Allen, who, though he presumably had had no formal training in teaching, possessed a fine natural gift in that direction. His blackboard drawings and way of explaining locomotive mechanism and the rule book were wholly admirable and no one could have covered the subjects better in the short time allowed. The next week we had to attend in the office of the Running Shed Foreman and I have a note that I was asked but one question, "What must you do when coming on the shed with an engine?" This was apparently a common question, for Mr. Allen had been at pains to see that all knew the right reply, which I gave: "See that all the points are pulled right over". The foreman then kept us an hour reminiscing on his career and stressing the virtues of sobriety, why I know not, for as far as I recall we all were and looked abstemious, though we went when we could to a nearby café called "Erne and Mabel's".

After passing as fireman at the end of November, I was still chiefly occupied in disposing, though another job was fireman to the "Shedturner", a driver who moved engines from one part of the shed to another and turned them on the table if necessary. This was good practice for learning the position of the points for the different roads, which was something one needed to be familiar with to avoid difficulties in fog or darkness.

As far as I can see from brief diary references, I had made only two trips out before Christmas, one to shunt at Curzon Street, the historic original terminus of the London and Birmingham, and the other to Aston Gas Works, where my driver was the husband of the local M.P. for that part of Birmingham, Mrs. Wills. With so little experience of work outside the shed, I was therefore woefully ill prepared for what befell me on Boxing Day.

On reporting for duty at 4.0 p.m., I was told that I would be firing a main line express passenger train from Birmingham to Crewe, for which the engine was class five 4–6–0 No. 4953. We picked up eight coaches at Vauxhall sidings, but through being held up outside New Street did not leave with the second portion of the 5.40 (due out at 5.50) till nearly an hour late. Thus there began for me what was, as it would be for anyone who had not graduated towards it by more conventional stages, one of the most memorable experiences of a lifetime. Once we had worked up to high speed, I learnt at one fell swoop something that no one who has not experienced it can appreciate; the great difference between the smooth riding of coaches and the lively motions of a locomotive. With the footplate vibrating and shaking as we rushed forward into the darkness, I found it impossible to stand without hanging on to something for most of the way and even when going more slowly could not get all my shovelfulls of coal through the firehole door, let alone into the right parts of the grate. Fortunately, I was with just about as good a driver as one could hope to have in these conditions. Of Freddie Gibbs it could be said as of "The Laughing Policeman" in the song, "A fat and jolly red-faced man, he really was a treat". Seeing that the job was pretty well beyond me, and probably having learnt in advance that I had not been on the main line before, he did the bulk of the firing himself, looking to see that the next signals were off and then getting down to put six round the box. And what is more, he did it most willingly and cheerfully.

Another thing one learns on a first high speed firing turn is the transformation it causes to the furnace. When shunting the fire burns up bright and red when

Large-boilered 'Claughton' 4–6–0 No. 5946 on a Liverpool-Chester train at Wavertree shortly after the war. The last survivor of these engines caused some difficulty on a visit to Aston. [*Eric Treacy*

Not a very practical engine for shunting: Webb "18 inch goods" 0–6–0 No. 8367 on a Cambridge-Bletchley train at Fenny Stratford. [*C. R. L. Coles*

the engine is steaming, but at continuous speed it becomes absolutely white and apart from the heat one might be looking at a mass of newly fallen snow. The grate has to be kept covered with coal at every point, or air rushes in and heat is lost; and the method of checking that no such holes in the fire are developing is to put the shovel on the lip of the firehole door and deflect air to cool each area into some kind of visibility. This too my mate had to do, for this trick needs experience.

Sharing the work between us, doing what I could when the riding was not too rough though losing a good deal of coal by catching the shovel on the sides of the firehole, and Mr. Gibbs making good the shortcomings, we reached Crewe at 8.15 and took the engine into the North Shed where she was based. A visit to the office revealed that there was no return trip for us to work—something of a relief to me, and no doubt to my mate—but that we should not be able to return to Birmingham till a quarter to one the next morning. With so long a wait and the prospect of going back as passengers, refreshments were called for and took up much of the time before the infinitely more comfortable run southwards.

It must have been the chronic shortage of firemen immediately after Christmas that led to my going on this run, but during the post-war period there must have been countless other instances of drivers being given firemen without the knowledge to do their work properly. The nation owes a debt of gratitude to these middle aged or elderly men who had to undertake not only their own task but also someone else's and yet manage to get their trains through.

The new year of 1947 brought a welcome widening of activity. After the rather boring weeks of disposing and the veritable slave driving of steam raising under busy conditions, it was pleasant to be put on a variety of different jobs with various drivers. Runs with both passenger and freight between Birmingham and Lichfield, Coventry, and two more to Crewe were intermixed with shunting at the Birmingham goods yards and at nearby stations like Stechford, Marston Green, and Adderley Park. Each place one visited had marked individuality, Adderley Park for instance in that the shunting neck was so situated that the shunter could not be seen and engine movements were directed by notes struck on a large bell inset on the blue brick wall adjoining the station. Another feature there was the prevalence of rats. Anyone getting down from the footplate in the quiet small hours of the morning would be sure to disturb these creatures and hear them scampering away into the darkness. Many a day proved most interesting and fascinating, especially if it involved fresh territory. Others could be boring, like being on the banking engine kept at Perry Barr to help push trains up the incline round the Handsworth loop and waiting for hours before anyone needed assistance. Most trying of all is to wait a long while in the middle of the night at a signal that is on and to have to concentrate on watching for it to change to green; the temptation to go to sleep is almost irresistible.

The winter of 1946 to 1947 was one of exceptional severity, the coldest for about one hundred years in parts of Britain, and of all the bitterly cold runs I made the worst was the return to Aston from Wichnor, the junction with the Midland Division. Aston had regular assignments to take empty trucks to that point and bring back trains of coal for the local gas works. At that time, a "Super D" (ex-L.N.W. 0–8–0) was always used. There was no provision for turning the engines at the end of the run, so all the way back from Wichnor we had to come tender first with the very inadequate protection of the low sided tender. Though buttoned up in a strong overcoat, I was much colder at the end of that trip than I had ever been in the previous years on the Atlantic or North Sea. Riding for miles into an icy wind, one saw how fully justified were the tender cabs fitted to some engines of this class in even more exposed parts of the country.

Not having been allocated to a regular link, my turns took me on to a wide variety of different types of engine. While the steam locomotive is highly individualistic and that there are good and bad ones in all classes (often for reasons which defy analysis), there are certain dominant characteristics which stick in my memory as the outstanding features of those I worked on. The Fowler 0–6–0 tanks or "Jinties", of which we had three numbered consecutively from 7363, seemed exceptionally free steaming and economical in coal consumption. Even when working quite hard on shunting, a mere six shovelfulls every twenty minutes kept the pressure up. The same designer's 2–6–2 tanks had more tendency than any others to lock their driving wheels and slide when shunting. Apart from this, the general view was that the later Stanier 2–6–2 tanks were much better engines, though it was held that with the 2–6–4 tanks there was little to choose between the creations of the two engineers. One class which could be guaranteed not to "pick up" their wheels under any conditions were the Webb goods engines known to enthusiasts as "Crestheads" or "Cauliflowers" but to enginemen always as "eighteen inches". These had by far the worst brakes of any class represented at Aston. When shunting with them and applying the brake, even full on, there seemed to be several revolutions of the wheels before any retardation could be perceived and then it took effect only very slowly. Another drawback they had for such work was a screw reverser with an unusually large number of turns to get from full ahead to full reverse; so a day's shunting with one was like a day's mangling. With good brakes and lever reverse, the somewhat older Midland 0–6–0s built by Johnson is the 1870s were much handier machines and our veterans like 3008 and 3196 had good big cabs as well. In dry, hot summer weather, especially if there were a breeze, the eighteen inches did have one fitting missed on the Midland engines, a pipe from which water could be sprayed on the coal to lay the dust. All Mr. Johnson laid on was a tap in the tender from which buckets of water could be filled for this purpose, a less effective method.

The Super Ds were extremely popular with drivers on account of their wonderful capacity to move heavy loads, but the peculiar arrangement of the footplate, which instead of being flat involved a depression in the centre with raised portions round it, made them awkward for the firemen. Further, the floor where one stood was of metal instead of the usual wood, so was potentially hazardous; the risk of slipping and going over the side was greater on these engines. Webb 0–6–2 coal tanks were nearly always used for coach marshalling at Vauxhall and showed their strength in handling heavy loads one might have thought beyond the capacity of such small engines. A coal tank would couple up to twelve coaches of an express which had made its main line journey and with great aplomb haul them out up the brick viaduct towards New Street, not slipping in spite of the gradient. The sudden convulsive effort, commendable as it was, could not have been kept up for long, however, for although starting with a gauge glass full of water, it would be bubbling around the bottom nut when the climb stopped and it was time to put on the injectors and set back slowly propelling the coaches into their sheds. The extension of the side tanks alongside the cab made these the least commodious of all for the crew, but one admired their pulling

Stanier 2–6–4T No. 2229 as running in 1948 [*T. Newbold*

power, even if it could not be long sustained with loads like this. We called them "Gadgets" and it was 27591 I knew best.

Just as the engines embraced a wide range of good and bad points, so did the drivers. Instead of having a regular mate as applied to those allocated to a permanent link, the disposing and control relief work that I did meant constant variations from week to week or even day to day. So I worked with many different drivers out of the dozens employed at Aston. They ranged between the jolly or sour, the idle or industrious, the tolerant or impatient, the chatty or dour. In general, however, those with attractive characteristics far outnumbered those without and one could not have wished for more pleasant and interesting company. Apparently firemen would not have been able to say that in the past, when these drivers had been handling the shovel. Several affirmed that in their younger days it was the custom for their drivers to be very stand-offish and to speak to firemen only when it was unavoidable. It was a good thing that by my time this tradition had largely disappeared, for if two people are to be together all day the more friendly their relationship the more pleasantly will the time pass.

On a visit to Aston in 1946: the unique 'Royal Scot' 4–6–0 No. 6170 "British Legion", rebuilt from the unsuccessful high-pressure engine "Fury".
[*O. H. Prosser*

The most entertaining drivers with whom to pass the time were those who would reminisce at length on the subject which they knew best, their past lives on the railway, nearly always the old North Western, for most had spent lifetimes at the same shed. Everyone suffers the temptation to glamorise the past; but in the case of the older enginemen of the 1940s however, they were speaking nothing but the literal truth when they said (as they all did) that in their early days they would never have believed that the sorry conditions they saw around them would ever come to pass. They recalled how as cleaners they had expended hours on ensuring that even freight engines were turned out glistening and spotless, whilst in the immediate post war period the only clean engine was one just out of shops from general repair. Not only were most L.M.S. engines by that time covered in rust and dirt but also the wheels were caked in so thick a coating of grease and oil that it used to be said that only this held them together. The rot had set in with the introduction of common user engines in the inter-War years, a method which through economic necessity, it was said, had had to replace that of keeping one engine for one crew. One driver used to relate how in the days when he was fireman of one particular Fowler 2–6–0 (or "Crab") when it was newly built, he visited the shed on Sunday mornings in his own time to give it special attention. Buying his own metal polish, soap and brushes, he would spend leisure hours burnishing all the footplate fittings and actually scrubbing the wooden floor of the cab! For those who had been brought up in a tradition of this kind it was naturally dispiriting to be surrounded by filthy and neglected machines.

In spite of the falling off in standards of cleanliness and the fact that the purchasing power of their pay was markedly less than it had been pre-War, most drivers liked their work and recognized its good points such as freedom from supervision and endless variety. All were agreed, however, that there was one drawback to life on the footplate which went far to outweigh its advantages: the irregularity of the hours of duty. Shift working with the twenty four hours of the day split into three eight hour periods is performed by hundreds of thousands of workpeople in many occupations and is not found too irksome by those who have to do it. Footplatemen are in a worse position than ordinary shiftworkers as they may have to start at any time of night or day. Variations ranging from starting in the small hours of the morning one week, followed by mid afternoons, say, the next, not only prevent one's following any normal pattern of living but also rule out much chance of pursuing social activities. Family life is also disrupted. As one driver put it, "When you're on this job, you're married to the railway and no one else".

Conscious as they were of how the bad hours limited pursuit of the other things that might have helped make life more worth living, most enginemen found an interest in their work which went far to compensate them for the fact that it left little time for anything else. This was shown by their willingness in regaling anyone who would listen with recollections of the past, tales such as how when one very short driver went by a signalbox he could not be discerned in the cab and the signalman reported a train running away out of control. Another was of how in an exceptionally cold winter a driver found himself unable to get down from the cab seat, having got frozen into a set position. Another sign of the interest of the staff in their craft lay in the very good attendances at the Mutual Improvement Class meetings in Birmingham. In spite of the absence of many who had to be on duty, the room was packed for such talks as I attended on exhaust steam injectors, oil firing of locomotives (then being extended through the current coal shortage), and the new colour light signalling layout for New Street Station and its tunnels. The last mentioned talk in particular, given by a Mr. Williams, one of the chief signal engineers of the L.M.S., showed that these meetings had a very real value in that there was a two-way flow of ideas. The audience was not merely a passive one, there to receive information imparted by the speaker. Instead, after dealing fully with the current plans for re-signalling, the speaker invited comments from the drivers who would have to observe the new arrangements. He received a number from the body of the hall, made copious notes from what was said, and undertook to revise certain plans in the light of what had been put to him. The railways must have benefited from this kind of workers' participation.

This eagerness for self improvement in the skill and knowledge which they could bring to bear in doing their work seemed thoroughly in keeping with the spirit of devoted and conscientious service that was typical of most enginemen. They were a grand crowd, doing their duty as best they could and cheerfully (or at least philosophically) accepting a sad deterioration in their conditions. When one reflects on the state of the shed, with slag heaps uncleared and fire irons in short supply, and of the engines often in poor mechanical condition, one feels that the tools with which the enginemen were supplied were unworthy of the men who used them. In 1946-47 and thereabouts they looked back to a golden past and accepted an indifferent present.

All this was a long time ago now. After twenty years, however, one has the advantage of a greater sense of perspective in recalling the past. One rejects fading, ephemeral impressions and remembers only those stamped indelibly on the memory. That is probably what J. B. Priestley had in mind when he said in his autobiography "Margin Released" that in trying to write of past events it is best to be separated from them by a long time. As it is, I recollect only part of the events and experiences which made up probably the most worthwhile and exciting ten months of my life. If I had my time over again, it is the period I should most look forward to re-living: and if one can honestly say that of an episode in life's story, it is a measure of the fascination which the glamour of the footplate cast on one who has never experenced anything else to compare with it.

Asthmatic but brute-forceful too
Neglected yet obedient
With rusty sides and clanking rods
Yet still alive and servient

She is doomed now: men condemn her
Say she's dirty and old-fashioned
Far too costly, and her service
Is a labour without profit

So go she must, and now instead
We'll have machines of greater power
The figures prove their better worth
In ton-miles per train engine-hour.

To those who believe that all figures are truthful
Her death will be welcome: but some will remember
Her power and her struggle, her grime and her glory.
Though gone like the sunset, she'll not be forgotten.